Nick Vandome

A Parent's Guide to the iPad

in
easy steps

2nd edition
covers iOS 6
for 3rd & 4th generation iPad and iPad 2

In easy steps is an imprint of In Easy Steps Limited
4 Chapel Court · 42 Holly Walk · Leamington Spa
Warwickshire · United Kingdom · CV32 4YS
www.ineasysteps.com

Second Edition

Notice of Liability
Every effort has been made to ensure that this book contains accurate
and current information. However, In Easy Steps Limited and the
author shall not be liable for any loss or damage suffered by readers
as a result of any information contained herein.

Trademarks
All trademarks are acknowledged as belonging to their respective
companies.

In Easy Steps Limited supports The Forest Stewardship Council (FSC),
the leading international forest certification organisation. All our titles
that are printed on Greenpeace approved FSC certified paper carry the
FSC logo.

MIX
Paper from
responsible sources
FSC® C020837

Printed and bound in the United Kingdom

ISBN 978-1-84078-588-3

Contents

1 Your Child Needs an iPad

For a parent, the thought of your child having an iPad can be a daunting one. Will they look after it? Will they use it productively? Will they be safe? This chapter introduces using an iPad with your child and shows some of the ways it can be used effectively.

The iPad Revolution

Apple Computers has the happy knack of turning the way we look at the world of computing on its head. The first most dramatic example of this was the introduction of the iMac: an all-in-one desktop computer that was so stylish that people wanted to have it on display rather than hide it away in a study or a spare bedroom. This was followed by the iBook and the MacBook: laptops that quickly featured in a range of hip and savvy television programs and films. But the two products that propelled Apple into the real mainstream of consumer electronics were the iPod and the iPhone. The iPod quickly became the number one MP3 device for playing digital music and the iPhone followed by taking the smartphone market by storm. The iPod and the iPhone ensured that Apple was no longer simply viewed as a manufacturer of computers, albeit very iconic ones.

The i What?

Following on from the success of its other i devices, Apple introduced the first iPad in January 2010. Initially, sceptics scratched their heads in a rather puzzled fashion: what was the iPad exactly? It seemed to lack the productivity to replace a traditional laptop and it was too large to be just a communications device. But, as is their habit, Apple had launched the right product at exactly the right time. The iPad is a tablet computer that is compact, has a longer battery life than a laptop and has a range of functionality for both work and entertainment. Because of its size, it is easily carried in a bag, or even a large pocket, and has Wi-Fi and, in some versions, 3G/4G connectivity to the Web. And of course the design has the usual Apple wow-factor and immediately makes people want to have one as soon as they see it. This, added to a number of celebrity endorsements, has ensured that, with the iPad, the era of the tablet computer has well and truly arrived.

Hot tip

If your iPad ever freezes, or if something is not working properly, it can be re-booted by holding down the **Home** and **On/Off** button for 10 seconds and then turning it on again (see page 24 for details of the controls on the iPad).

Don't forget

In October 2012 the iPad Mini was introduced, which is a 7.9-inch version of the iPad, as opposed to the standard 9.7-inch version.

A Perfect Match

For adults, who have grown up with the evolution of the desktop PC, the iPad can initially seem like something of a strange beast – it is almost too good at what it does; being able to handle most computing tasks while still being stylish and compact. But for children it is a perfect match. Untainted by the times when computers only came in beige boxes, today's children are used to mobile computing devices that let them communicate, study and play in as easy a way as possible. In this respect the iPad ticks all of the boxes. Also, being a style icon does no harm in terms of its appeal to children.

Some of the areas in which the iPad is ideal for children are:

Beware

iPads are not inexpensive so safeguards should be taken to prevent them being lost or stolen from you child. See Chapter Three for more information about physical security.

- **Appearance.** In an era where brand is more important than ever before, the name Apple is one of the most recognizable among children. The iPad is seen as something that children are more than happy to show to their peers and, rather than being seen as a dull computer, it is much sought-after, partly because of its stylish appearance and its brand appeal

- **Battery life.** Children have busy, active lives and they do not want to have to worry about constantly charging their mobile devices. With a battery life of up to 10 hours, the iPad ensures that frustration with recharging is kept to a minimum

- **Size.** The iPad is compact enough to be put in a jacket or a school bag and big enough to be used effectively for most computing tasks

- **Apps.** The iPad comes with a range of its own apps (programs) and there are thousands more that can be downloaded from the App Store. These cover everything from entertainment to education. Some of them are free while others have to be paid for. But there will almost certainly be an app for whatever interests your child

Using an iPad

Any parent, grandparent or teacher who is responsible for a child using an iPad will want to know exactly what can be done with it. Because of its versatile nature this may depend on the child's creativity and inventiveness, but the using the iPad can be broken down into two main categories:

- Using iPad apps
- Using App Store apps

iPad apps

iPad apps are those that come pre-installed with the iPad. These can be accessed from the icons on the iPad Home screen:

Hot tip

To download apps from the App Store, the user will need an Apple ID. Since some apps have to be paid for, it is best if this is set up, and administered, by an adult rather than give control of it to a child. See page 21 for details about obtaining an Apple ID.

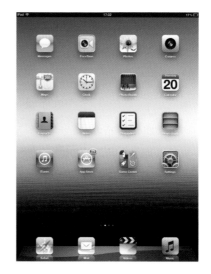

- **App Store.** This can be used to access the App Store, from where additional apps can then be downloaded

- **Calendar.** An app for storing appointments, important dates and other calendar information. It can be synced with iCloud

- **Clock.** This can be used to view the time in different countries and also as an alarm clock and a stopwatch

- **Contacts.** An address book app. Once contacts are added here they can then also be accessed from other apps, such as Mail

- **FaceTime.** This is an app that uses the built-in FaceTime camera on the iPad to hold video chats with other iPad users, or those with an iPhone, iPod Touch or a Mac computer

- **Game Center.** For those who like gaming, this is an app for playing a variety of games, either individually or with friends

- **iBooks.** This is an app for downloading electronic books, that can then be read on the iPad. This can be done for plain text or illustrated iBooks. Although this is considered a built-in app, it has to be downloaded from the App Store first

- **iTunes.** This app can be used to browse the iTunes store where music, TV shows, movies and more, can be downloaded to your iPad

- **Mail.** This is the email app for sending and receiving email on your iPad

- **Maps.** Use this app to view maps from around the world, find specific locations and get directions to destinations

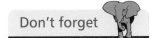

Don't forget

To use FaceTime the other user has to have iOS 5, or later, on their iPad, iPhone or iPod Touch or OS X Lion (7.2 or later) on their Mac.

Hot tip

Items in apps including Calendar, FaceTime, Game Center, Mail, Messages and Reminders can be flagged up in the Notification Center. This is accessed by dragging downwards from the top of the iPad screen.

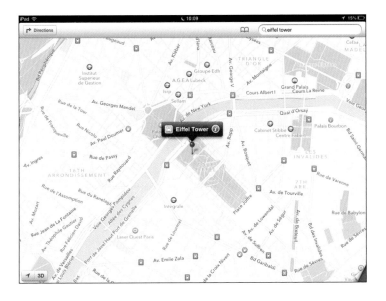

- **Messages.** This is the iPad messaging service, that can be used between iPads, iPhones, iPod Touches and Mac computers. It can be used with not only text but also photos and videos

11

...cont'd

● **Music.** An app for playing music on your iPad and also viewing cover artwork. You can also use it to create your own playlists

● **Newsstand.** Similar to iBooks, this app can be used to download and read newspaper and magazine subscriptions

● **Notes.** If you need to jot down your thoughts or ideas, this app is just perfect for that

● **Photo Booth.** A photography app that can be used to create distorted and special effects photos of people or objects

● **Photos.** This is an app for viewing and editing photos and creating slideshows

● **Reminders.** Use this app for organization, when you want to create to-do lists and set reminders for events

● **Safari.** The Apple Web browser that has been developed for viewing the Web on your iPad

● **Videos.** This is an app for viewing videos on your iPad and also streaming them to a larger HDTV monitor

Using an iPad Together

Once your child has an iPad there will be many occasions when they will want to use it on their own, for either studying, playing games or communicating with their friends. However, you should try to ensure that it is not solely a solitary pastime: try to develop the feeling that using the iPad can also be a shared experience. This can help you understand how your child is using the iPad and you can also discuss any potential problems. Talk openly about what you expect the iPad to be used for and aim to create mutual trust about a balance between using it as  a study tool and also an entertainment center. But most of all, try to make sure that you and your child can make using the iPad together an enjoyable experience.

When you are using the iPad with your child there are some areas you should think about:

- Offer support and help when needed but be prepared to take a back seat if your child is coping well without your help. Try not to take over, even if you think you know best

- Be prepared to learn yourself. It is sometimes a hard fact to accept, but there are times when our children know more than we do! So look forward to learning new skills and embrace the chance to let your child teach you

- Talk openly about potential problem areas. These could include inappropriate websites and issues about talking to strangers on message boards. If you can talk honestly about these things then your child is more likely to come to you if there is a problem

Hot tip

Try to find a shared interest with your child on the iPad, such as a hobby you can research, or a game you can play together and compare your scores.

13

An Education Tool

In terms of exactly what an iPad should be used for, there may be some divergence of opinion between parents and their offspring: with the former championing it as an education tool and the latter favoring it as a games and communications device. However, the good news is that the education elements of the iPad can be a lot of fun in themselves, so a happy compromise should be easy to achieve. There are two ways in which the iPad can be used as an education tool:

- **Productivity apps.** These are apps that can be used for producing, saving, sharing and printing school work

- **Learning apps.** These are education apps that can be used for learning for all ages

Productivity apps

The three main apps for this are:

- **Pages**, for word processing

- **Numbers**, for spreadsheets and databases

- **Keynote**, for presentations

These apps can be downloaded from the App Store and files can also be saved into formats compatible with Microsoft Office programs, Word, Excel and PowerPoint.

Don't forget

Pages, Numbers and Keynote have to be paid for, but they are less expensive than their Microsoft Office counterparts.

Don't forget

For more information about using productivity apps, see Chapter Six.

Learning Apps

Learning apps can be downloaded from the App Store and there is a huge range of them, covering all age groups.

Pre-school children are catered for with early-learning apps covering reading, writing and counting.

For older children there are apps for all of the main subjects that are likely to be studied at school.

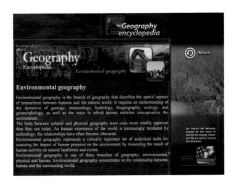

An Entertainment Tool

When a child picks up an iPad their first port of call may not be an app to do their English or science homework (but hopefully this will come later). Instead they are more likely to focus on the entertainment functions available. These fall broadly into two categories:

- **Media.** Apps for accessing photos, music and videos

- **Games.** There thousands of games apps that can be downloaded from the App Store. These can be played independently, or through the Game Center app

Media

For viewing and editing music, photos and video, the apps with the same name can be used. These apps can display graphical covers when playing music and create artistic slideshows for viewing photos.

Hot tip

You can connect an iPad to a large screen HD television for viewing videos or photos.
This is done by attaching an Apple Digital AV Adapter (Lightning or 30-pin connector), which is sold separately.

16

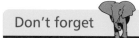
Don't forget

For more information about using photo, music and video apps, see Chapter Seven and Eight.

Apps such as iTunes and Photos can also be used to download music from the iTunes Store and edit photos respectively.

Game Center

The pre-installed Game Center app enables you to play a range or games, either by yourself or with like-minded people with an iPad, iPhone or iPod Touch. This will link to a game-playing network where you can compare scores against individuals or join a multiplayer game.

App Store Games

The App Store has a range of games for all tastes and ages. Browse through them on the Games category page or type in a keyword in the search box to find a specific game.

Don't forget

Within the Games category there are sections for New & Newsworthy, What's Hot and What We're Playing.

Don't forget

For more information about using games apps, see Chapter Eight.

A Window to the World

No computer, or mobile device, is complete without access to the Internet and the Web. On the iPad this is provided by the Safari Web browser app. This provides standard access to the Web, but with one main difference for the traditional computer user.

What, no mouse?

The iPad has no mouse, something that may confuse users from the generation that grew up with this ubiquitous pointing device. However, times move on and the navigation on the iPad is done by a collection of taps, swipes and pinching gestures. These are know as Multi-Touch Gestures and they are used to navigate Web pages within Safari. Two of the main areas are:

Scrolling

To move up and down Web pages, swipe in the opposite direction to the one in which you want the page to move:

Zooming

To zoom in on an item on a Web page, pinch outwards with thumb and forefinger (or double-tap with one finger):

Don't forget

All of the navigation on an iPad is done with Multi-Touch Gestures and these are looked at in detail in Chapter Two.

Beware

Multi-Touch Gestures can take a bit of getting used to, so don't panic if you cannot get the hang of them immediately. However, children tend to take to them with great ease.

Communicating with an iPad

The younger generation live in a world in which they expect to be fully connected with their friends in a range of digital ways: phone, text, email, messaging (text and video) and social networking. The iPad caters for most of these needs so that your child is only ever a click away from their friends.

Mail

This is the email app on the iPad. An account can be set up with the free Apple iCloud service or settings for an existing account can be added.

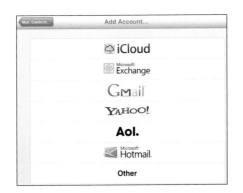

Beware

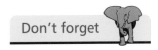

Sometimes you can get too much of a good thing and so some forms of communications by your child may need to be monitored. This can include messaging and social networking in particular.

When receiving email, attachments can be viewed directly within mail without having to open them separately.

Don't forget

For more information about using Safari and Mail on the iPad, see Chapter Nine.

iMessages

This is the text messaging service on the iPad that can be used for free with other iPad, iPhone and iPod Touch users. It works with the Messages app, over Wi-Fi or 3G/4G networks, and messages can also include photos and videos that you have on your iPad.

Conversations can be held with individual people:

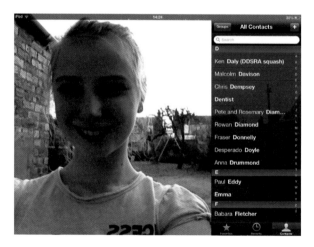

FaceTime

FaceTime is an app that enables you to make video calls over Wi-Fi or 3G/4G networks with other iPad, iPhone, iPod Touch or Mac computer users. You have to sign in with an Apple ID (see next page) and an email address and once you have done this you can then make video calls:

The FaceTime camera is the one facing you when you are looking at the screen. The other camera on the iPad cannot be used for FaceTime calls.

Don't forget

Text messages in Messages are typed with the virtual keyboard that appears when you are ready to create a new text message.

Don't forget

For more information about using Messages and FaceTime on the iPad, see Chapter Nine.

20

Obtaining an Apple ID

An Apple ID is a registered email address and password with Apple that enables you to log in and use a variety of Apple services. These include:

- App Store
- iTunes Store
- iCloud
- iMessage
- FaceTime
- Game Center
- iBooks

It is free to register for an Apple ID and this can be done when you access one of the apps or services which requires this, or you can do it on the Apple website at My Apple ID:

1 Tap once on the **Create an Apple ID** button

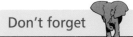
Create an Apple ID

2 Enter your email address and a password

Create an Apple ID.

Choose an Apple ID and password.
Enter your primary email address as your Apple ID. This will be used as the contact email address for your account. Please note that this email address must be verified before you can use certain Apple services.

Apple ID	@mac.com
Password	••••••••
Confirm Password	••••••••

Create a security question.
Select a security question or create one of your own. This question will help us verify your identity should you forget your password.

3 Enter additional details such as date of birth and address. Enter the security code and tap once on the **Create Apple ID** button

Please type the characters you see in the image below.

QCTGR

↻ Try a different image
◀) Vision Impaired

QCTGR
Letters are not case sensitive.

☑ I have read and agree to the Apple Terms of Service and Apple Customer Privacy Policy.

Cancel   Create Apple ID

Security Overview

There is almost no limit to the ways in which an iPad can be used for education, entertainment and communication. However, for any parent, grandparent or teacher, one of the main concerns will be security. This falls into two main categories:

- **Physical security.** This covers ensuring, as much as possible, that your child's iPad is not lost or stolen

- **iPad security.** This covers what can, and cannot, be done on the iPad and the Web

Physical security

Some areas to bear in mind once your child has an iPad are:

- **Where is it going to be used?** If the iPad is only going to be used in the home then this represents less of a security risk. However, if it is going to be taken to different places then some consideration should be taken about how to keep it safe

- **If it is being carried around is it inconspicuous?** Since an iPad is a small, and valuable, item it can be an easy target for anyone trying to steal it. Therefore it is advisable to keep it out of view when it is being carried around

- **Is it insured?** Insurance can be obtained for an iPad when you buy it or it may be covered by household insurance. However, check any policies carefully to ensure that they provide sufficient cover

iPad security

Within the **Settings** app of the iPad are a number of restrictions that can be applied to a range of apps and content:

Don't forget

For an in-depth look at security and restrictions, see Chapter Three.

Allowed Content:	
Ratings For	United Kingdom >
Music & Podcasts	Explicit >
Movies	All >
TV Shows	All >
Books	All >
Apps	All >
In-App Purchases	ON
Require Password	15 minutes >

2 Getting to Know the iPad

Even if your child is going to be the main user of the iPad, it is still important for you to understand its functions and capabilities. The iPad operates differently from a traditional computer and this chapter takes you around the hardware and software that makes up the iPad. After getting used to this, and seeing how powerful it is and how much it can do, you may want to use it yourself too.

Around the iPad

The controls for the iPad are simple and uncomplicated. Three of them are situated at the top of the iPad and the other is in the middle at the bottom. There are also two cameras, one on the front and one on the back of the iPad.

Controls
The controls at the top of the iPad are:

On/Off button

Side Switch for silent mode (this applies to system sounds rather than the volume of items such as music or videos)

Volume Up or **Down** button

Cameras. One is located on the back (iSight), underneath the On/Off button and one on the front top (FaceTime HD)

Home button. Press this once to wake up the iPad or return to the Home screen at any point

Don't forget

The fourth generation iPad has an iSight camera on the back, which is a 5-megapixel camera and can also capture video in HD. The other camera is a FaceTime 1.2 megapixel HD camera, for use with the FaceTime app for video calls.

Beware

iPads do not have any USB ports or DVD/CD drives. If you want to transfer items from an iPad this generally has to be done by sending them by email, sharing them with iTunes or the online Apple service, iCloud. For more details about sharing files, see Chapter 10.

Speaker. The speaker is located here on the bottom of the iPad:

Lightning cable connector. Connect the dock cable here to charge the iPad, connect it to an iPad Dock, or another computer. (iPad 2 and the third generation iPad come with a 30-pin connector. See tip on page 25.)

Specifications

The current version of the iPad is the fourth generation and there are two main models of the 9.7-inch screen version, one with 4G connectivity (where available, but also covers 3G), for connecting to a mobile network, and one without. Apart from this, the specifications are the same:

- **Height:** 9.50 inches (241.2 mm), width: 7.31 inches (185.7 mm), depth: 0.37 inch (9.4 mm), weight 1.44 pounds (652 g)

- **Processor:** Dual-core Apple A6X with quad-core graphics

- **Storage:** 16GB, 32GB or 64GB of in-built flash storage

- **Wireless:** Wi-Fi (802.11a/b/g/n; 802.11n on 2.4GHz and 5GHz), Bluetooth 4.0

- **Screen:** Retina display, 9.7-inch (diagonal) LED-backlit glossy widescreen Multi-Touch display with IPS technology, 2048-by-1536-pixel resolution at 264 pixels per inch (PPI), fingerprint-resistant oleophobic coating

- **Battery power:** Up to 10 hours of surfing the Web on Wi-Fi, watching video, or listening to music

- **Battery charging:** Via power adapter (supplied) or USB to computer system

- **Input/Output:** Lightning connector port, 3.5 mm stereo headphone minijack, built-in speaker, microphone and micro-SIM card tray (Wi-Fi + 4G model only)

- **Sensors:** Accelerometer, ambient light sensor and gyroscope

- **TV and video:** AirPlay Mirroring to Apple TV support at 720p, video mirroring and video out support: up to 1080p with Apple Digital AV Adapter or Apple VGA Adapter (adapters sold separately)

- **Mail attachment support:** The following file formats can be opened or viewed through the Mail app: .jpg, .tiff, .gif (images); .doc and .docx (Microsoft Word); .htm and .html (web pages); .key (Keynote); .numbers (Numbers); .pages (Pages); .pdf (Preview and Adobe Acrobat); .ppt and .pptx (Microsoft PowerPoint); .txt (text); .rtf (rich text format); .vcf (contact information); .xls and .xlsx (Microsoft Excel)

Don't forget

In addition to the standard 9.7-inch iPad, there is also a 7.9-inch iPad Mini version. This runs on the same operating system (iOS 6) as the full-sized version and can use all of the same apps. It also has the same options in terms of storage and Wi-Fi specifications, but weighs approximately half the amount of the larger version. Also, the iPad Mini does not have a Retina display screen.

Beware

The fourth generation iPad comes with the new lightning connector. So, you'll need to buy adapters to connect it to your "old" 30-pin accessories, such as TV, iPod dock, etc.

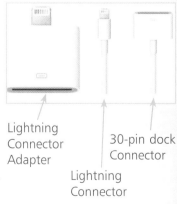

Lightning Connector Adapter

30-pin dock Connector

Lightning Connector

Setting Up

To start using the iPad, press the **On/Off button** once and hold it down for a few seconds.

Initially there will be a series of setup screens to move through before you can use the iPad:

 Drag this slider to the right to start the setup process (This is done by dragging the slider with one finger.)

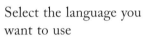 Select the language you want to use

After each step, tap once on this arrow in the top right-hand corner, or the **Next** button

4 Select the country in which you are using the iPad

5 Tap once here to enable Location Services. This will enable certain apps on the iPad to identify specific locations for where you are

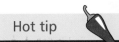

Hot tip

If Location Services is enabled it can be used in conjunction with the Find My iPad function, if it is lost or stolen. Location Services can then identify where the iPad is.

6 If you are using a Wi-Fi network to connect to the Internet, tap once on one of the available networks. You will then need to put in a password for the network, or your router if you are using your own network

...cont'd

7 Tap once here to set up the iPad as a new device

Set Up as New iPad	✓
Restore from iCloud Backup	
Restore from iTunes Backup	

8 Tap once here to use a current Apple ID or create a new one. This can then be used to access the iCloud service. This is a function that allows you to share items such as photos, music, apps and documents across other Mac computers and mobile devices

Don't forget

The iCloud service automatically syncs items on your iPad with any other iCloud-enabled devices. This includes other Mac computers, iPads, iPhones and iPod Touches, which can then share content from your iPad, such as music, photos and documents.

9 Tap once here to start using the iCloud service

10 Tap once here to back up items on your iPad to the iCloud service

11 Tap once here to activate the Find My iPad service. This can be used to locate the iPad if it is lost or stolen

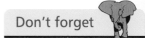

Don't forget

For more about setting up and using Find My iPad, see Chapter Three.

12 Tap once here to send diagnostic information automatically about the iPad to Apple

29

13 Drag this button to the right to register your iPad with Apple

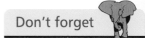

Don't forget

It is always a good idea to register your iPad so that you are established as its owner and also so that you can get regular software updates.

14 Tap once here to start using the iPad

First View

Once you have completed the setup process you will see the Home screen of the iPad. This contains the built-in iPad apps:

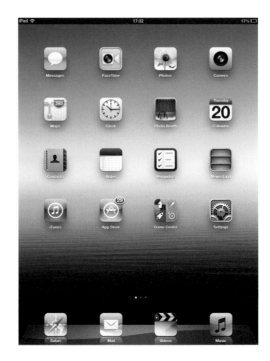

At the bottom of the screen are four apps that appear by default in the Dock area. Tap once on any app on the Home screen to open it:

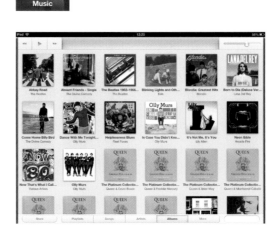

Home Button

The Home button, located at the bottom, middle on the iPad, can be used to perform a number of tasks:

1. Click on the **Home button** once to return to the Home screen at any point

2. Double-click on the **Home button** to access the Multitasking Bar. This shows the most recently-used and open apps. The rest of the Home screen is grayed out. Tap once on an app to access it

Hot tip

The Multitasking Bar can also be accessed by swiping upwards from the bottom of the iPad with four fingers.

3. Click once on the **Home button** when on the Home screen to access the iPad search function

Hot tip

To close an open app, tap and hold on it on the Multitasking Bar until it starts to jiggle and a red circle appears in the top left-hand corner. Tap once on the circle to close the app. This does not delete it from the iPad though.

Screen Orientation

Content on an iPad can be viewed in either portrait (vertical) or landscape (horizontal) mode. To do this, rotate the iPad and the content will be adjusted accordingly.

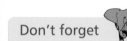

Don't forget

Content on the iPad rotates 360 degrees, so as you keep rotating it the content will appear in the correct orientation.

Locking screen rotation

If you do not want the iPad screen to rotate every time that you move it, it is possible to lock it in position. This can be done in two ways:

1 Double-click on the **Home button** to access the Multitasking Bar

2 Swipe from left to right

3 Tap once here so that the lock icon appears, to lock the screen rotation

or

1 Tap once on the **Settings** app

2 Tap once on the **General** tab

3 Under **Use Side Switch to**: tap once on **Lock Rotation**

4 Push the **Side Switch button** down so that the orange dot is showing, to lock screen rotation

Hot tip

The buttons on the Multitasking Bar next to the lock button can be used to, from left to right, adjust the screen brightness, control video and music playback and adjust volume.

Items on the Dock

The apps on the Dock at the bottom of the screen can be rearranged in any way you require. The default ones are put there as it is thought they are the most commonly-used. However, you can add and remove them. To do this:

1 To remove an app from the Dock, tap and hold it and drag it onto the main screen area

2 To add an app to the Dock, tap and hold it and drag it onto the Dock

3 The number of items that can be added to the Dock is restricted to a maximum of six as the icons do not resize themselves

System Settings

The Settings app is the one that should probably be explored first as it controls settings for the appearance of the iPad and the way it, and its apps, operate. To use the Settings app:

1 Tap once on the **Settings** app

2 The Settings are listed down the left-hand side and the options are shown on the right-hand side

3 Tap on a link to see additional options for that item

4 Tap once here to move back to the main category for the selected Setting

...cont'd

The System Settings are:

● **Airplane Mode.** This can be used while on an airplane and switches off the wireless and cellular receivers

● **Wi-Fi.** This enables you to select a wireless network. Available networks will be displayed here

● **Bluetooth.** Turn this On to connect Bluetooth devices

● **Do Not Disturb.** Use this to specify times when you do not want to receive audio alerts or FaceTime video calls

● **Notifications.** This determines how the Notification Center operates in terms of alerting the user to different types of notifications

● **General.** This contains a number of settings for how the iPad operates. This is one of the most useful Settings

● **Sounds.** This contains options for setting sounds for alerts for items such as mail and calendar items

● **Brightness & Wallpaper.** This can be used to set the screen brightness manually or automatically and select a wallpaper

Brightness & Wallpaper
Auto-Brightness ON
Wallpaper

● **Picture Frame.** This can activate your iPad as a picture frame when it is locked

● **Privacy.** This can be used to activate Location Services so that your location can be used by specific apps

● **iCloud.** This contains settings for items that are to be saved to the online iCloud

● **Mail, Contacts, Calendars.** This has options for how these three apps operate

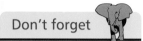

Don't forget

Within the Notification Center you can turn On or Off items which you want to appear here. The Notification Center is accessed by dragging downwards from the top, middle of the screen.

- **Notes.** This contains formatting options for creating items in the Notes app

- **Reminders.** This has an option for syncing your reminders for other devices, covering a period of time

- **Messages.** This can be used to sign in to the Messages app for sending and receiving text messages

- **FaceTime.** This is used to turn video calling On or Off

- **Maps.** This contains options for displaying distances in miles or kilometers in the Maps app and also the way labels are displayed on maps

- **Safari.** Settings for the Safari Web browser

- **iTunes & App Stores.** This can be used to specify downloading options from the iTunes Store and the App Store, for music, books and apps

- **Music.** This has options for how you listen to music

- **Videos.** This has options for how you view videos

iTunes & App Stores
Apple ID: nickvandome@mac.com

iTunes Match	OFF

Store all your music in the cloud with iTunes Match.
Learn more...

Automatic Downloads

Music	OFF
Apps	OFF
Books	OFF

Hot tip

When you start downloading new apps from the App Store, some of these will appear in the Settings section, if they have options that can be edited, such as using iCloud for storing items.

37

- **Photos & Camera.** This has options for viewing and editing photos, slideshow settings and options for uploading to iCloud, using Shared Photo Streams

- **iBooks.** This contains options for reading books in the iBooks app, including hyphenation and using bookmarks

- **Newsstand.** Use this set of options to download new content for items in the Newsstand app automatically

- **Twitter.** Use this to install Twitter and create an account

- **Facebook.** As above, but for Facebook

iOS 6

The operating system for the iPad, i.e. the software that makes everything work, is known as iOS 6. This is an operating system for mobile devices and is also included with the iPhone. Details about the operating system can be found within the Settings app. To view the iOS 6 details:

1 Tap once on the **Settings** app

2 Tap once on the **General** tab

3 Tap once on the **About** link

About	>

4 Details about the iPad are displayed. This includes information about what is stored on the iPad, its capacity and available capacity, the version of the OS, the iPad model, serial number and wireless addresses

Don't forget

You can change the name of the iPad in the About section.

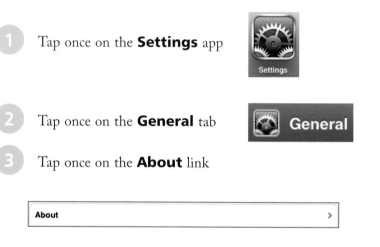

5 Tap once on the **Software Update** link

Software Update	>

6 Details about the current version of the OS are displayed

iOS 6.0.1
Your software is up to date.

Don't forget

If there is a newer version of the iOS 6 software available it will appear in the Software Update section.

7 Tap once on the **Usage** link

Usage	>

8 Details about what has been stored on the iPad are displayed and also the available iCloud storage

General	Usage	
Storage		
2.4 GB Available		11.5 GB Used
Photos & Camera		1.2 GB >
GarageBand		1.1 GB >
Videos		1.1 GB >
iBooks		1.0 GB >
Numbers		375 MB >
Pages		325 MB >
Show all Apps		
iCloud		
Total Storage		25.0 GB
Available		23.8 GB
Manage Storage		>
Battery Usage		
Battery Percentage		ON

Beware

Children can be in the habit of downloading a lot of music, photos and videos, if they are given the chance. This can quickly fill up the storage capacity of the iPad.

Finding Things with Siri

Siri is the iPad voice assistant that provides answers to a variety of questions by looking at your iPad and also Web services. You can ask Siri questions relating to the apps on your iPad and also general questions, such as weather conditions around the world, or sports results. Initially, Siri can be set up within the Settings app:

1 In the General section, tap once on the **Siri** link

2 Drag the Siri button to **On** to activate the Siri functionality. Tap once on these links to select a language, set voice feedback and allow access to your details

Hot tip

Using explicit language with Siri can be blocked within **Restrictions** in the **General** section of the **Settings** app. See Chapter Three for more details about setting restrictions.

40

Questioning Siri

Once you have set up Siri, you can start putting it to work with your queries. To do this:

1 Hold down the **Home button** until the Siri window appears

Hot tip

Siri can be used to open any of the built-in iPad apps, simply by saying, **Open Photos**.

2 To find something from your iPad apps, ask a question, such as **Show me my reminders**

Siri can also find information from across the Web and related Web services:

1 Siri can provide sports results, for certain sports in certain countries, such as in response to the question **How did Barcelona get on in their last match?**

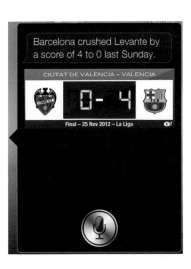

2 Weather reports are another of Siri's strong points and and it can provide weekly forecasts in response to the question, such as **What is the weather like in Tokyo?**

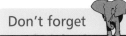

Don't forget

Siri has a certain amount of personality and can add its own editorial comments to certain types of queries.

3 However, even Siri's knowledge is limited and if there is a subject it does not recognize it will own up and offer to search the Web instead

The iPad Keyboard

The keyboard on the iPad is a virtual one, i.e. it appears on the touch screen whenever text or numbered input is required for an app. Settings for the keyboard can be determined in the General section of the Settings app. To do this:

1 Tap once on the **Settings** app

The keyboard appears automatically whenever you tap on an item to perform any input task, such as word processing, emailing, entering a Web address or entering details in an online form.

2 Tap once on the **General** tab

3 Tap once on the **Keyboard** link

Keyboard >

4 Drag the sliders to **On** or **Off** to enable or disable the relevant functions

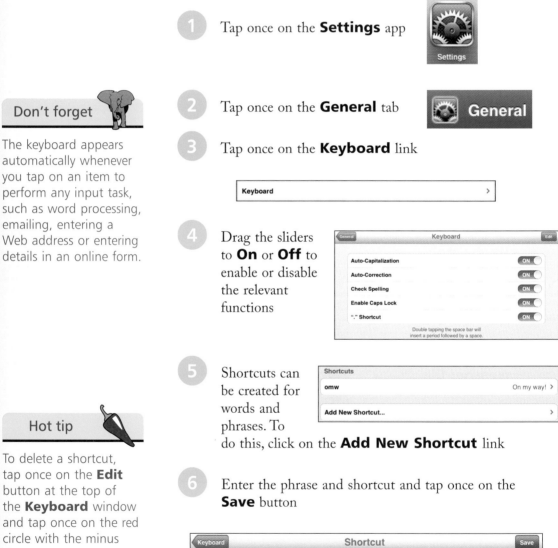

General | Keyboard | Edit

Auto-Capitalization — ON

Auto-Correction — ON

Check Spelling — ON

Enable Caps Lock — ON

"." Shortcut — ON

Double tapping the space bar will insert a period followed by a space.

5 Shortcuts can be created for words and phrases. To do this, click on the **Add New Shortcut** link

Shortcuts

omw — On my way! >

Add New Shortcut... >

Hot tip

To delete a shortcut, tap once on the **Edit** button at the top of the **Keyboard** window and tap once on the red circle with the minus sign inside next to a shortcut to delete it.

6 Enter the phrase and shortcut and tap once on the **Save** button

Keyboard | Shortcut | Save

Phrase laugh out loud

Shortcut lol

Create a shortcut that will automatically expand into the word or phrase as you type.

Undocking the keyboard

By default, the keyboard is docked at the bottom of the screen. However, it is possible to undock it so that it appears higher up the screen. To do this:

 Press and hold on this button on the keyboard

Tap once on the **Undock** button

Drag on the button in Step 1 to move the keyboard around the screen

Splitting the keyboard

The keyboard can also be split into two and used on either side of the screen. To do this:

Press and hold on this button on the keyboard

Tap once on the **Split** button

The split keyboard can be moved around the screen in the same way as undocking it, by clicking on the button in Step 1

Hot tip

The button for undocking and splitting the keyboard can also be used to hide it, by tapping on it once.

Don't forget

To unsplit and redock the keyboard, press and hold on the button in Step 1 and tap on the **Dock and Merge** button.

Don't forget

For more information about entering and formatting text with the keyboard, see pages 116–117.

Multi-Touch Gestures

Since there is no mouse connected to the iPad, navigation is done with the user's fingers. There is a combination of tapping, swiping and pinching gestures that can be used to view items such as Web pages, photos, maps and documents and also navigate around the iPad.

Swiping up and down

Swipe up and down with one finger to move up or down Web pages, photos, maps or documents. The content moves in the opposite direction of the swipe, i.e. if you swipe up, the page will move down and vice versa.

Tapping and zooming

Double-tap with one finger to zoom in on a Web page, photo, map or document. Double-tap again to return to the original view.

Pinching and swiping

Swipe outwards with your thumb and forefinger to zoom in on a Web page, photo, map or document.

Pinch together with your thumb and forefinger to zoom back in.

Pinch together with your thumb and four fingers to return to the Home screen from any open app.

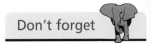

Don't forget

Swiping outwards with your thumb and forefinger enables you to zoom in on an item to a greater degree than double-tapping with one finger.

45

More gestures

- Swipe left or right with four or five fingers to move between open apps

- Swipe up with four or five fingers to reveal the Multitasking Bar at the bottom of the screen

- Drag with two or three fingers to move a web page, photo, map or document

- Swipe left or right with one finger to move between full-size photos in the Photos app

- Tap once on a photo thumbnail with one finger to enlarge it to full screen within the Photos app

- Tap once with two fingers on a full-size photo to reduce it to a thumbnail within the Photos app

- Drag down at the top-middle of the iPad to view current notifications in the Notification Center

Hot tip

The gestures involving four or five fingers can be turned **On** or **Off** in the **General** section of the **Settings** app.

iPad Smart Cover

One of the issues with a touch screen, such as the one on the iPad, is that it is liable to get scratched if it is carried around in a bag or even being moved around in the home. The solution to this is an iPad cover. Being Apple, this not only protects the screen but is designed so that it can also be used as a stand to support the iPad for viewing content or typing with the keyboard.

There is a setting for the iPad cover in the Settings app. This can enable it to lock or unlock the iPad:

 Tap once on the **Settings** app

Tap once on the **General** tab

Under **iPad Cover Lock/ Unlock** drag the button to **On** to enable the cover to lock or unlock the iPad when it is placed in position or removed

Attaching the cover
The iPad cover attaches with a hinge along the left-hand side of the iPad. Attach it by placing the hinge on the side of the iPad until it clicks into place:

Using the cover as a stand

The iPad cover is separated into four foldable panels. These can be folded into a triangular shape to create a stand for the iPad:

Use the stand at the top of the iPad when using the keyboard for input options:

Use the stand at the bottom of the iPad when viewing content such as videos, photos, books or magazines:

Accessories

The iPad is perfectly equipped to be used on its own, without any accessories. However, accessories can not only be fun to add, they can also be functional. Some possible iPad accessories include:

- **Wireless keyboard.** This is an Apple product that is intended primarily for the iMac computer. However, it can be linked to an iPad via Bluetooth and it is a useful option if the iPad is going to be used for a lot of typing, e.g. for essay writing

Hot tip

The wireless keyboard has to be 'paired' with the iPad. This is done by turning **On** Bluetooth in the **Bluetooth** Setting. Under **Devices**, the keyboard will then be recognized and paired.

- **Camera accessories.** If you want to download photos from your own digital camera this can be done with two iPad accessories: a camera connector and a SD card reader. Both of these plug into the slot at the bottom of the iPad where the power cable is attached. The camera connector enables you to download photos and videos directly from a camera while the SD card reader can be used to download content from any SD memory card

- **iPad Dock.** This is a stand that can be used to position the iPad for viewing content and it can also be used to charge the iPad and connect it to external speakers

- **Digital AV Adapter (Lightning connector or 30-pin connector).** This can be used to connect your iPad to a HDTV screen so that you can view photos and videos on a large screen. With this adapter the same content on the iPad is played on the TV screen

- **Apple TV.** This is another way of viewing content from your iPad on your TV. Instead of a cable connection, this is done by streaming video and photos wirelessly to the Apple TV box which then plays it on the TV

Don't forget

Apple TV can also be used to download and view content from the iTunes Store, such as movies and TV shows.

3 iPad Security

Online and physical security are two of a parent's main concerns if their child has an iPad. This chapter details some of the potential dangers and offers advice about combating them. From safer social networking, to iPad restrictions, this chapter covers some issues to put your mind at rest.

Areas of Concern

The biggest concern for a parent or teacher of a child with an iPad is that it will be used inappropriately, either by the child themselves or by someone else contacting them via the Web. This falls into two main categories:

- Viewing of inappropriate material
- Contact by strangers on social networking sites, email or messaging sites

Restricting access

Children have always tried to read, look at and watch material that is not necessarily appropriate for their age group. To a degree this is unavoidable but, unfortunately, the Internet has significantly multiplied the amount of inappropriate material that is available. Moreover, a lot of it is significantly beyond the boundaries of what can be considered acceptable.

As shown later in this chapter, there are restrictions that can be put in place to prevent access to certain types of content. But children can be endlessly inventive when it comes to doing things that they shouldn't and nothing is ever completely secure in the world of computing. There may be occasions when they come across inappropriate material, whether it is through online sites with Safari or content in iTunes. Rather than bar these areas completely a good compromise is to put some restrictions in place and discuss with your child what is, and is not, acceptable. You should also have access to the iPad so that you can see what is being viewed: if your child doesn't want to do this it could be an indication that they have something to hide.

Stranger danger

Social networking sites are great for children to keep in touch with their friends, but they can also be a minefield in terms of strangers contacting children, usually under the guise of being their contemporaries. Relationships can then be formed, with the child thinking it is with someone of their own age when the reverse could be true. Also, adults can convince teenage children to meet them or even persuade them to leave home with them.

Dangers on the Internet will never go away but if you are aware of them then you should be able to prevent your child falling prey to some of the malicious practises that are out there.

Beware

It is essential that your child does not form online relationships with people who they do not know, even if the other person claims to be a friend of a friend. If in doubt, your child should be encouraged to tell you about anything with which they are uncomfortable or unsure, no matter how trivial it may seem.

Physical Security

An iPad is a valuable and expensive piece of equipment, particularly for a child to have, so it is important to try to ensure that it is as safe as possible when it is in their possession. This falls into two categories:

- **Safety in the home** – making sure the iPad doesn't get damaged or broken

- **Security outside the home** – making sure the iPad doesn't get lost or stolen

In the home

When your child is using the iPad in the home there are a few rules that should be followed to keep the iPad in good condition:

- **Drinks.** Liquid is the enemy of any piece of electrical equipment so all drinks should be kept well clear of your iPad

- **Hands.** Children have a habit of getting dirty and sticky hands. Make sure that they are always washed, and dried, before your child uses the iPad

- **Cables.** If the iPad is plugged into anything (for charging or transferring files) make sure that the cables are away from feet and legs, so that they do not get caught up

Away from home

There will be many occasions when your child will want to take the iPad away from home, either to use with their friends or to take to school. Some issues to consider about this:

- **Plain bag.** Keep it as inconspicuous as possible and carry it in a plain bag so that it is out of sight

- **Know the serial number.** If the iPad is lost or stolen make sure you know the serial number so that you can quote this if it is found. This is located within the **General > About** section of the Settings app, under Serial Number

- **Keep it with you.** Stress to your child the importance of keeping the iPad with them. Do not give it to other people or leave it unattended in a bag

- **Report any loss.** If the iPad is lost or stolen, ensure that your child tells you as soon as possible so you can take any action

Hot tip

A lot of companies offer specific insurance for iPads and you should also check to see if it is covered by your home and contents insurance.

51

Finding Your iPad

If the worst comes to the worst and your iPad is lost or stolen, help is at hand. The Find My iPad function (operated through the online iCloud service) allows you to send a sound alert to a lost iPad and also remotely lock it or even wipe its contents. This gives added peace of mind, knowing that even if your iPad is lost or stolen its contents will not necessarily be compromised.
To set up Find My iPad:

1 Tap once on the **Settings** app

2 Tap once on the **iCloud** link

3 Drag this button to **On** to be able to find your iPad on a map and send messages to it remotely

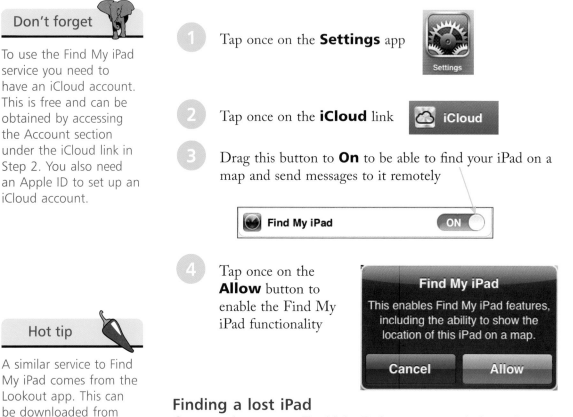

4 Tap once on the **Allow** button to enable the Find My iPad functionality

Finding a lost iPad

Once you have set up Find My iPad you can search for it through the online iCloud service. To do this:

1 Log in to your iCloud account at **www.icloud.com**

2 Tap once on the **Find My iPhone** button (this also works for the iPad)

3 Tap once on the Devices button and select your iPad. It is identified and its current location is displayed on the map

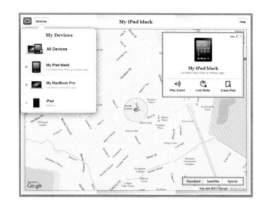

4 Tap once on the green circle to view details about when your iPad was located

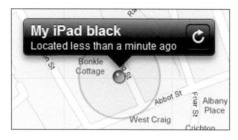

5 Tap once here to send a sound alert to your iPad

Hot tip

Tap once on the Erase iPad button in Step 5 to delete the contents of your iPad so that no-one else can access them.

6 Tap once here to lock your iPad remotely

7 Enter a passcode so that no-one else can access the contents on your iPad

53

Locking Your iPad

If you are worried about your iPad falling into the wrong hands, and its information being compromised, it is possible to set a passcode so that no-one can access the contents of the iPad without the correct code. To do this:

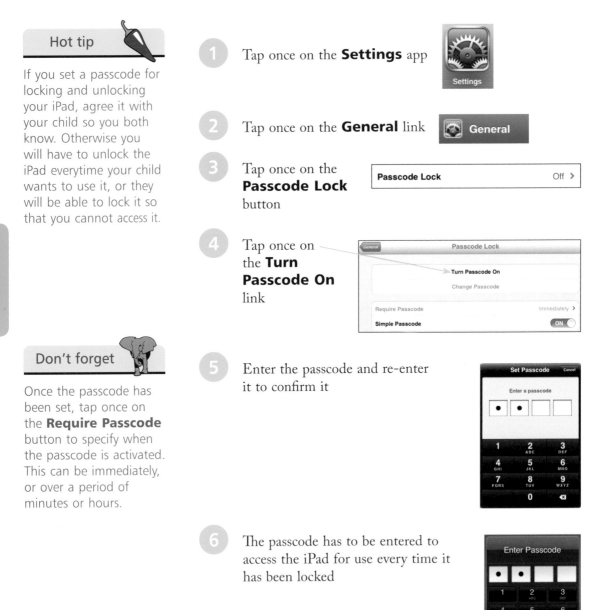

Hot tip

If you set a passcode for locking and unlocking your iPad, agree it with your child so you both know. Otherwise you will have to unlock the iPad everytime your child wants to use it, or they will be able to lock it so that you cannot access it.

Don't forget

Once the passcode has been set, tap once on the **Require Passcode** button to specify when the passcode is activated. This can be immediately, or over a period of minutes or hours.

1 Tap once on the **Settings** app

Settings

2 Tap once on the **General** link

General

3 Tap once on the **Passcode Lock** button

Passcode Lock   Off >

4 Tap once on the **Turn Passcode On** link

General   Passcode Lock
Turn Passcode On
Change Passcode
Require Passcode   Immediately >
Simple Passcode   ON

5 Enter the passcode and re-enter it to confirm it

6 The passcode has to be entered to access the iPad for use every time it has been locked

Viruses

As far as security from viruses on the iPad is concerned there is good news and bad news:

- The good news is that, due to its architecture, most apps on the iPad do not communicate with each other so, even if there were a virus, it is unlikely that it would infect the whole iPad. Also, there are relatively few viruses being aimed at the iPad, particularly compared to those for Windows PCs

- The bad news is that no computer system is immune from viruses and malware and complacency is one of the biggest enemies of computer security. Also, as iPads become more popular, and more widely used, they become a more attractive target for hackers and virus writers

iPad security

Apple takes security on the iPad very seriously and one way that this manifests itself is in the fact it is designed so that different apps do not talk to each other. This means that if there was a virus in an app then it would be hard for it to transfer to others and therefore spread across the iPad. Apple's own apps are the exception to this, but as they are developed and checked by Apple there is very little chance of them being infected by viruses.

Apple also checks apps that are provided through the App Store and this process is very robust. This does not mean that it is impossible for a virus to infect the iPad (but there have not been any so far) so keep an eye on the Apple website to see if there are any details about iPad viruses.

Antivirus options

There are few apps in the App Store that deal with antivirus issues, although not actually removing viruses, due to the lack of iPad viruses in circulation. Some options to look at:

- **VirusBarrier.** This checks files that are copied onto your iPad, via email or online services, to ensure that they are virus-free

- **McAfee Global Threat Intelligence Mobile.** This is not technically an antivirus app, but it does provide a daily update about new viruses that are in circulation

- **Anti-Virus Detective.** This is an app that has a step-by-step process to go through to identify suspected viruses or malware

Online Security

Organizations for online security

The issue of online security for children is taken extremely seriously by governments and police forces around the world. There are police taskforces to monitor exploitation on the Internet and organizations that offer advice and help.

One site that offers a range of advice about safety on the Web is the Child Exploitation and Online Protection Centre. Their website can be found at **ceop.police.uk**:

Tap once on this icon to access the CEOP Internet Safety Centre

This has advice for all age groups and also a link to report problems directly to CEOP:

CEOP also has its own age-specific websites (Thinkuknow) covering Web safety, while still being able to get the most out of your Web experience. Each of the age-specific sites can be accessed from the CEOP homepage.

Some of the key issues dealt with by sites like CEOP are:

- Know how your child is accessing online content and, if possible, have them do this somewhere in the home where you are, so that it is not a secret

- Talk to your child about the issues to do with online safety and also how they use the Web. Create a partnership in terms of Web use and generate an atmosphere of trust with your child so that they can feel confident and secure when accessing content on the Web. Using the Web should be fun and this involves both you and your child feeling secure and confident about their online activities

- Encourage your child to tell you anything with which they are unhappy or unsure. Reassure them that they will not get into trouble for doing this and that it is never wrong to flag up something they are concerned about

- Know how to report your own concerns. Either do this directly on a website, or to your child's school, through CEOP or, ultimately, to the police. No matter how trivial you think something may seem, it is always worth reporting it if it makes you uneasy or you think there is the possibility that someone is acting inappropriately towards a child online

Don't forget

CEOP has a list of links to other useful sites concerned with child safety on the Web.

Social Networking Safety

Safety on social networking sites, particularly Facebook, can be a major concern for parents and teachers. Talk to your child about this as much as possible and be open with each other about your concerns and views. Some of the main issues to consider are:

- There is a 13 year-old minimum age for having a Facebook account. However, there is no way for the site to enforce this and so the only realistic way is through parental control. Despite this it would still be possible for children under 13 to open an account at their friends' houses or other locations. So, in some ways, if a younger child is asking for a Facebook account it is sometimes better to allow this so that you can have some control over what they are doing. Obviously, some judgment will be required about what is too young, but it is best to have some flexibility and agreement.

- If you have your own Facebook account it is perfectly possible to be friends with your own child. They may have their own views on this but it can be a good compromise for children under 13 particularly. However, even if you are friends with your child they will still be able to communicate with their peers via private messaging

- Never become friends with someone you don't know. It is relatively easy to set up fake Facebook accounts and pretend to be someone that you are not. If you get a friend request from someone you don't know, then don't accept it

- Never advertise parties or social gatherings at your home. A lot of small social gatherings have been hijacked via Facebook and turned into chaotic parties

- Things that are on Facebook can stay there permanently if they are not removed. Some employers now search the Facebook pages of prospective employees to see if there is anything untoward there. This can go back several years

- Nothing is private. Photos and comments can be copied and distributed to people via other means, such as email. Even private messages can be copied

- Even if you are annoyed with someone, don't post inappropriate comments about them. This can quickly get out of control and cause a lot of problems for all concerned

Beware

Cyberbullying is one of the main concerns on the Web and particularly on social networking sites. Encourage your child to tell you about anything that is upsetting or worrying them. However, children can also be bullied, and feel excluded, if they are not part of the social networking community.

Beware

Always make sure that you log out of your Facebook account whenever you are away from your iPad. If not, someone could access your account and post messages pretending to be you. This is known as a 'frape', which is a contraction of 'Facebook rape'. Even if this is done in a humorous way, it can cause huge problems among children.

Safer Browsing

The default browser for web content on the iPad is Safari. However, the Mobicip Safe Browser can be downloaded from the App Store to ensure safer browsing for children. To do this:

Download the Mobicip app and tap once on this button

When you first access the app you have to register with Mobicip. At this point you can also apply settings for your child. You can also do this by accessing the Mobicip website at **www.mobicip.com**
Tap once on the Add Another User button

Enter the name of your child and tap here to specify their school level

Once in the Mobicip browser, tap once here and tap on the **Settings** link

Tap once on a child's name to enable them to use the browser. You have to log in to your account each time you want to change a user

If inappropriate content is attempted to be accessed, this message appears

Hot tip

Within the Mobicip browser, tap once on this button on the bottom toolbar to access the Mobicip homepage, where there are links to child-friendly websites.

Restrictions

Within the iPad Settings there are a number of options for restricting types of content that can be viewed and also actions that can be performed. These include:

- Turning off certain apps so that they cannot be used

- Enabling changes to certain functions

- Restricting content that is viewed using specific apps

When setting restrictions, they can be locked so that children cannot change them back or set them themselves. To do this:

1. Tap once on the **Settings** app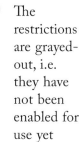

2. Tap once on the **General** link

3. Tap once on the **Restrictions** link

Allowed Content:	
Ratings For	United Kingdom >

4. The restrictions are grayed-out, i.e. they have not been enabled for use yet

Allow:	
Safari	ON
Camera	ON
FaceTime	ON
iTunes	ON

5. Tap once on the **Enable Restrictions** link

Enable Restrictions

6 Type on the keypad to set a passcode for enabling and disabling Restrictions

7 Re-enter the passcode

8 All of the Restrictions options become available

Beware

If you forget the passcode for unlocking your iPad it will become disabled for a period of time after you have entered the wrong passcode a number of times. Eventually, it will lock completely.
It can be reset by using a computer with which the iPad was last synced and there are details about this on the Apple website Support pages. However, to avoid this, ensure that you have a note of the iPad's passcode, but keep it away from the iPad itself.

61

Allow:

Safari	ON	
Camera	ON	
FaceTime	ON	
iTunes	ON	
iBookstore	ON	
Installing Apps	ON	
Deleting Apps	ON	
Siri	ON	
Explicit Language	ON	

Allowed Content:

Ratings For	United States >
Music & Podcasts	Explicit >
Movies	All >
TV Shows	All >
Books	All >
Apps	All >
In-App Purchases	ON
Require Password	15 minutes >

Allowing Apps

One of the biggest security concerns for parents or teachers of children using an iPad is that they will use certain apps to access inappropriate content or use them for activities such as messaging or video chatting with strangers. If you are concerned about this, certain apps can be turned off so that they cannot be used at all. To do this:

1 Access the Restrictions section as shown on the previous two pages

2 Drag these buttons to turn a specific app **On** or **Off**

Allow:	
Safari	OFF
Camera	ON
FaceTime	ON
iTunes	ON

Don't forget

If an app is turned off, it retains any settings that have been applied to it, e.g. bookmarks in Safari will still be there if you turn the app back on.

3 When an app is turned off it is removed entirely from the Home screen

Mail   Videos   Music

4 This option also enables you to turn the ability to install

Installing Apps	OFF
Deleting Apps	OFF

and delete apps on or off. If this is turned off then no new apps can be installed from the App Store, or deleted from the iPad

Allowing Changes

These restrictions enable you to turn on or off whether the iPad's location can be used for certain functions and whether changes can be made to Mail, Contacts and the Calendar apps. Generally the location option gives more functionality to certain apps, such as maps, and it is generally a useful thing to have turned on. To enable these changes:

1 Access the **Restrictions** section

2 Select an option under **Privacy** to allow changes for specific apps. Select **Accounts** under **Allow Changes** to allow changes in **Mail, Contacts and Calendars**

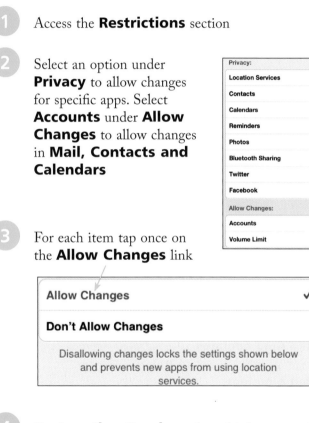

Privacy:	
Location Services	>
Contacts	>
Calendars	>
Reminders	>
Photos	>
Bluetooth Sharing	>
Twitter	>
Facebook	>
Allow Changes:	
Accounts	>
Volume Limit	>

3 For each item tap once on the **Allow Changes** link

Allow Changes	✓
Don't Allow Changes	

Disallowing changes locks the settings shown below and prevents new apps from using location services.

4 For **Location Services**, drag this button to **On** to enable Wi-Fi hotspots to identify the location of the iPad when you are using the iPad in a different location

Location Services	ON

Location Services uses crowd-sourced Wi-Fi hotspot locations to determine your approximate location.

Don't forget

For Location Services, each app that depends on a location is listed and can be turned on or off accordingly.

Allowing Content

Another parental concern about children using an iPad is about striking the right balance between letting them get as much benefit out of it, while ensuring that they do not view inappropriate content. One way to do this is to restrict the type of content that is available to view. This is done by selecting an appropriate ratings system for your location and then specifying the type of content that can be viewed for music, movies, TV shows and apps. To do this:

1 Access the **Restrictions** section

2 Under **Allowed Content**, tap once on the **Ratings For** link

Allowed Content:	
Ratings For	United States ❯

Don't forget

You should select the country in which you are located, but experimenting with other countries is a good way to see the types of movie and TV ratings they have.

3 Tap once on the country for which you want the ratings to apply

Ukraine	
United Arab Emirates	
United Kingdom	✓
United States	
Uruguay	

4 Tap once on the **Restrictions** button to go back (this should be done after each restriction item has been selected)

5 Tap once on the **Music & Podcasts** link

Music & Podcasts	Explicit >

6 Drag this button to **Off** to block any music or podcasts from the iTunes Store with explicit content

Allow Music & Podcasts Rated

EXPLICIT	OFF

Allow Playback of Music, Music Videos and Podcasts containing Explicit Content.

7 Tap once on the **Movies** link

Movies	All >

8 The movie ratings system for the country selected in Step 3 is displayed. Tap once on the rating up to which you want content to be displayed. The ones after it will then be blocked

Allow Movies Rated

Don't Allow Movies	
U	✓
PG	✓
12	✓
15	
18	
Allow All Movies	

Don't forget

Music and podcasts with explicit content are marked appropriately within the iTunes Store. However, if this is turned off within Restrictions Settings, these items cannot be played even when previewed in the iTunes Store.

...cont'd

9 Tap once on the **TV Shows** link

TV Shows	All >

10 Tap once on the rating up to which you want content to be displayed

Allow TV Shows Rated	
Don't Allow TV Shows	
CAUTION	✓
Allow All TV Shows	

Don't forget

In-App purchases consist of apps that contain additional content that has to be purchased. For instance, you may download a free painting app that has some free samples to use to paint over. There may then be additional samples that have to be purchased. Games frequently have in-app purchases.

11 Drag this button to **Off** to block any In-App Purchases

In-App Purchases	OFF
Require Password	15 minutes >

12 If In-App Purchases are turned On, tap once on the **Require Password** link and set an option for when a password has to be entered if buying In-App Purchases.

Restrictions	**Require Password**
Immediately	
15 minutes	✓

4 Apps and the App Store

Apps are the lifeblood of the iPad and enable you to do everything on it, from work to play and everything in between. This chapter shows how to use iPad apps and download new ones.

Introducing the App Store

While the built-in apps that come with the iPad are flexible and versatile, it really comes into its own when you connect to the App Store. This is an online resource and there are thousands of apps here that can be downloaded and then used on your iPad, including a wealth of both education and entertainment apps.

To use the App Store, you have to first have an Apple ID. This can be obtained when you first connect to the App Store. Once you have an Apple ID you can start exploring the App Store.

Don't forget

For details on how to obtain an Apple ID see Chapter One.

1 Tap once on this icon on the Home screen

2 The latest available apps are displayed on the home page of the App Store, including the iPad App of the Week

Beware

The content in the iPad App Store is not identical to that available from Apple computers, the iMac and MacBooks. While some of the apps are the same, they are developed specifically for the different systems.

3 Tap on these buttons to view the apps according to these headings

4 Tap on these buttons to view items according to these categories

| All Categories | Games | Education | Newsstand | More |

Viewing Apps

Once you have accessed the App Store you can then start exploring the apps that are available:

1   Tap once on an app

2   General details about the app are displayed

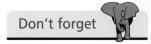

Don't forget

By default, the App Store opens on the Featured items page.

3   Swipe left or right here to view additional information about the app and view details from it

Don't forget

For more information about finding apps, see pages 72–74.

4   Ratings and reviews are available at the bottom of the page

Downloading Apps

When you identify an app that you, or your child, would like to use it can be downloaded to your iPad. To do this:

1. Find the app you want to download and tap once on this button (this will say Free or have a price)

2. The button changes to say **Install App**. Tap on this once

3. Enter your Apple ID details and tap once on the **OK** button

4. The app will begin to download on your iPad

5. Once the app is downloaded tap once on it to open and use it

Categories of Apps

Within the App Store apps are separated into categories according to type. This enables you to find apps according to particular subjects. To do this:

1 Tap once on the **More** button on the toolbar at the bottom of the App Store

2 The categories are listed alphabetically

Hot tip

New apps are added to all categories on a regular basis, so keep checking back to see what is new.

3 Tap once on a category to see the apps within it

Finding Apps

As well as looking through apps in specific categories you can also find them in other ways too.

Top Chart
To find the top paid for and free apps:

 Tap once on the **Top Charts** button on the toolbar at the bottom of the App Store

 The top overall paid for and free apps are displayed

To find the top apps in different categories, tap once on this button

Tap once on a category

The top apps for that category are displayed

Genius

This is a feature which suggests similar apps to those you have already downloaded. To use this:

1. Tap once on the **Genius** button on the toolbar at the bottom of the App Store

2. Tap once on the **Turn On Genius** button

3. Enter your Apple ID details as on page 70

4. **Agree** to the Terms and Conditions

5. Tap once on the **Done** button

6. Relevant recommendations will then appear in the Genius window once you have started downloading apps

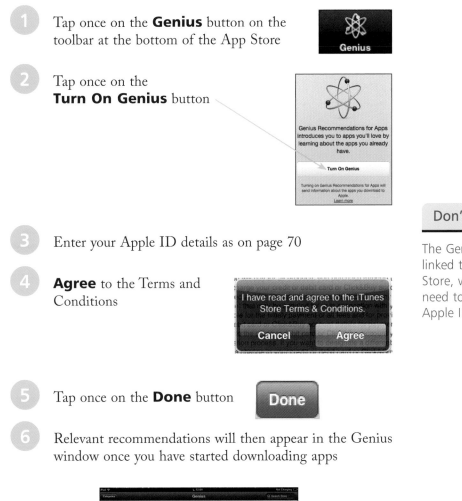

The Genius feature is linked to the iTunes Store, which is why you need to log in with an Apple ID.

Don't forget

73

...cont'd

Searching for apps

Another way to find apps is with the App Store Search box, which is located at the top-right corner of the App Store window. To use this:

Hot tip

When searching for apps, the results are displayed with an iPad Apps button and an iPhone Apps button at the top of the window. Tap on the iPhone Apps button if you do not see what you are looking for under iPad apps. These apps can also be used on an iPad.

Don't forget

By default, apps are sorted by **Relevance**.

1 Tap once in the **Search** box to bring up the iPad keyboard

2 Enter a search keyword or phrase

3 Suggested apps appear as you are typing. Tap once on an app to view it

Sorting

Within search results it is possible to sort the apps according to specific criteria. To do this:

1 Select an item from the search results as above

2 Tap once on these buttons to sort the suggested apps according to these criteria

3 Tap once on one of the buttons to view the sort options

Organizing Apps

When you start downloading apps you will probably soon find that you have dozens, if not hundreds, of them. You can move between screens to view all of your apps by swiping left or right with one finger.

Hot tip

To move an app between screens, tap and hold on it until it starts to jiggle and a cross appears in the corner. Then drag it to the side of the screen. If there is space on the next screen then the app will be moved there.

As more apps are added it can become hard to find the apps you want, particularly if you have to swipe between several screens. However, it is possible to organize apps into individual folders to make using them more manageable. To do this:

Don't forget

As in real life, children can sometimes prefer downloading apps rather than organizing them. So, from time to time, you may need to create some new folders to keep the Home screen tidy. Think of it as tidying a virtual bedroom!

1. Press on an app until it starts to jiggle and a white cross appears at the top-left corner

2. Drag the app over another one

...cont'd

Beware

Only top-level folders can be created, i.e. sub-folders cannot be created within the main one.

Hot tip

If you want to rename an apps folder after it has been created, press it until it starts to jiggle. Then tap on it once and edit the folder name as in Step 5.

 A folder is created, containing the two apps

 The folder is given a default name, usually based on the category of the apps

Tap on the folder name and type a new name if required

Click the **Home button** once to finish creating the folder

Click the **Home button** again to return to the Home screen (this is done whenever you want to return to the Home screen from an apps folder)

The folder is added on the Home screen. Tap on this once to access the items within it

Updating Apps

The world of apps is a dynamic and fast-moving one and new apps are being created and added to the App Store on a daily basis. Existing apps are also being updated, to improve their performance and functionality. Once you have installed an app from the App Store updates can be downloaded free of charge. To do this:

 When an update is available it is denoted by the red icon on the App Store button, showing how many updates are available

 Tap once on the **App Store** button

 In the App Store, tap once on the **Updates** button

 The available updates are displayed

Don't forget

When updates are available the red icon on the App Store button will appear automatically so that you will always know when there are new updates.

K12 Periodic Tabl... Version 2.2.3 04 October 2012	Updated to be compatible with iOS6 and the iPhone 5.	UPDATE
British Journal of... Version 2.0 08 November 2012	Completely rewritten reader - loads pages more quickly, with no low-res previews. iOS6 support and improvements.	UPDATE
Atomic Web... Version 7.0.1 20 November 2012	✓ Support for iOS 6 and iPhone 5 ✓ Cleaned up themes. ✓ Moved progress bar inside the address bar... **More▼**	UPDATE
Skype for iPad Version 4.1.1 11 October 2012	Fix for iOS 6 calling and video issues	UPDATE

 Tap once on the button next to an app to update it

 Tap once on the **Update All** button to update all of the required apps

Deleting Apps

If you decide that you do not want certain apps anymore, they can be deleted from your iPad. However, they remain in the iCloud so that you can reinstall them if you change your mind. This also means that if you delete an app by mistake you can get it back from the App Store without having to pay for it again. To do this:

1 Press on an app until it starts to jiggle and a white cross appears at the top-left corner

2 Tap once on the white cross to delete the app. In the Delete dialog box, tap once on the **Delete** button

3 Tap once on the **App Store** button

4 Tap once on the **Purchased** button

5 Apps that have been deleted have this iCloud icon next to them

6 Tap once on the **iCloud** button to reinstall an app

5 Educational Apps

The world of education is usually enthusiastic about embracing new technology and this is certainly true of the iPad. There is now a whole range of educational apps for all ages. This chapter shows the types of apps that can be used by both pre-school and high school children.

Using Educational Apps

For many adults, who have grown up thinking that all education involves using a pen and paper, the idea of using a gadget such as an iPad for educational purposes may seem a little frivolous. But times change and not only are children beginning to use mobile devices for all aspects of their lives, education establishments are now starting to use iPads and apps in mainstream education. As a parent, it is a revolution that cannot be avoided so it is best to embrace it with open arms and try to help your child get the most out of the iPad for educational purposes.

The rules have changed

Due to the multimedia nature of the iPad, the way in which it can be used for education is different from more traditional methods of classroom learning. For the older generation, education was usually done in two separate ways:

- Books, paper and pens for learning

- Toys for learning through play

With apps on the iPad these two methods are usually combined so you have a mixture of traditional learning methods, incorporated with games, puzzles and quizzes. Add in photos, videos and animations and it is easy to see why the iPad can be such an attractive learning tool for children.

Try out the lite version

Since there are thousands of education apps available it can sometimes be overwhelming trying to find the best ones for your child. One option for this is to try the lite version of an app. This is a free version of a paid-for app. The lite version only has some of the functionality of the full app but it will give you a flavor of it so that you can have a good idea about whether you want to buy the paid-for version or not. Lite versions of apps are usually identified with the word Lite on their icons within the App Store:

Working with Your Child

It is important that you are involved with any learning activities that your child is doing on the iPad. Obviously, this does not mean that you have to do everything with them, all of the time, and the age of your child will determine to some extent the amount of parental input. For younger children you will probably want to go through the learning process with them, while as they get older yours may become a more advisory role. Some of the ways that parents, grandparents or teachers can be involved are:

- Help find the best educational apps. You can do some research into this on your own but ultimately the best option is to find them with your child too

- Provide help and guidance where required. You should be up to speed on what each educational app offers so that you can help use the app and also discuss the subject matter

- Review work and learning outcomes that have been undertaken. A lot of apps have tests and quizzes so you can see how your child is dealing with the subject

- Know when to step back and let your child get on with things on their own. In any learning environment there is a fine line between providing assistance and being overbearing. Try to be there when needed but allow your child their own space to explore different apps at their own pace

Getting the right apps

When choosing educational apps, there may be some initial disagreement between you and your child: you may want the ones that look like they have the most educational benefit, while your child may gravitate towards the ones that look the most fun. Thankfully, with the majority of the iPad educational apps, the learning and the fun elements are combined so it should be easier to reach a consensus about the best apps to use. Since your child is the one who is going to be using the app the most, it is only reasonable to let them have their own input into obtaining apps. There may be times when you will have to compromise and go with their choice.

It is also a good idea to talk to your child's teacher when choosing apps. They may have some ideas of their own and they will be able to make suggestions based on what is being taught at that time.

Don't forget

The majority of educational apps are generally inexpensive so you should not spend a fortune even if you use several of them.

Following School Curricula

One area of great interest to parents and teachers will be the ways in which an iPad can be used to complement the work done for the school curriculum, particularly with a view to sitting exams.

Depending on your geographic location, there may be a range of apps that are specific to your country's education system. Some of these may be linked into existing websites that offer resources for your education system.

Finding relevant material

If you search for apps based on your country's education system you will be able to see any apps that are available for this. For instance, apps for the K–12 system, which is used in the USA, Canada and most parts of Australia, can be found by entering this as a search keyword:

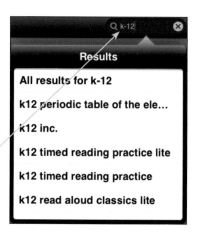

Apps can cover the whole education system in general or you could search for specific years, such as K–5:

For the UK, enter keywords relevant to the exams that are taken, i.e. GCSEs, A Levels, Standard Grades or Highers

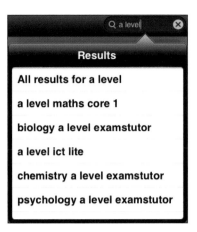

For A Level students there is a range of apps that are linked to the Examstutor website. This is an online learning resource that can be found at **www.examstutor.com**

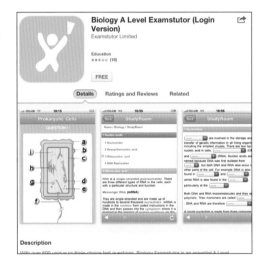

Hot tip

Some apps for A Level subjects have to be accessed from the iPhone Apps button in the Apps Store. However, they can also be used on the iPad.

The apps mirror the content on the main website and require the login details that the students use when they log in to the main site

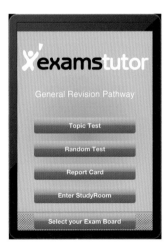

About Pre-School Apps

For children under school age there is a range of educational apps designed to start teaching them the basics of reading, writing and arithmetic. There are also apps for skills such as drawing and painting.

Pre-school apps are located in the main Education category in the App Store and can be found in a variety of ways:

1 Enter appropriate keywords into the Search box

2 Relevant suggestions are made based on the keywords. Tap on one of the suggestions to view that app

or

1 Tap once on the **Top Charts** button at the bottom of the App Store window

2 Tap once on the **All Categories** button and select **Education**. Within the top apps some are appropriate for pre-school or kindergarten children

Don't forget

Icons for pre-school apps are usually in the form of cartoon art so they are easy to recognize when being viewed alongside other apps.

Assessing apps

Once you have found an app in which you are interested:

1 Tap on it once

2 Read the description and view the details to assess whether you think it will be appropriate

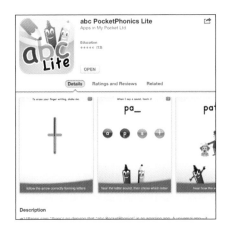

Some pre-school apps also have parental guides, or a parent zone, that can be ordered once you have downloaded the app itself. These offer advice about using the app with your child and how to get the most out of the learning experience with them.

Pre-School Apps

The following is a selection of pre-school apps covering reading, writing, counting and learning games. There are hundreds of other similar apps – the ones here indicate the range that is available and also the type of functionality they provide.

PocketPhonics
This is an app for learning to write. To use it:

Don't forget

Pre-school apps usually have buttons to take you back to the homepage, or a main menu, such as this one:

1 Tap once on this icon

pocketp...cslite

2 Tap once on the **Play** button

3 Tap once on a letter

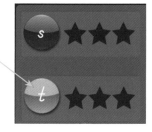

4 The letter is displayed and the app shows how to write it. Audio narration accompanies this

Say then watch how to write.

5 Drag over the letter with a finger to write it yourself on the iPad

Write with your finger.

TapToTalk

This is an app for learning to talk. To use it:

 Tap once on this icon

 Tap once
on one
of the
categories

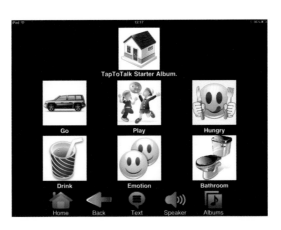

 Tap once
on an item.
The phrase
appears at
the top and
is spoken
by the
app. The
audio can
be turned
off so that
your child
can say the phrase for themselves

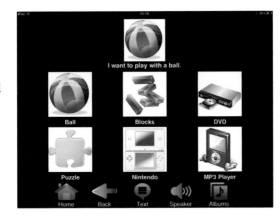

 Tap on these buttons to go to the home page, go back one
page, turn off text or audio and go to the albums section

...cont'd

Kids Math Fun

This is an app for learning basic arithmetic. To use it:

 Tap once on this icon

 Tap once on either the **Addition** or **Subtraction** buttons

A lot of mathematics apps have games and scores to make the learning activities more fun. This is also a good way to judge your child's progress with the app.

 A sum for the selected activity is displayed. Tap once on a number to select it for the answer

 A green tick appears if the answer is correct. Tap once on the Next button to move to the next sum

ABC SpellingMagic

This is an app for learning to spell. To use it:

1. Tap once on this icon

2. Select settings for the app and tap once on this arrow to start the app

3. Tap once on a letter item

4. An item and its letters are displayed, including boxes for the letters

5. Drag the letters into the boxes to create the word. Tap once on the arrow to move to the next word

...cont'd

Pre-School Classroom

This is an app for learning a range of skills, including reading, writing, arithmetic and matching items. To use it:

1 Tap once on this icon

2 Tap once on this button (or the **Play** button)

Don't forget

Most pre-school apps have an option for adding your child's name as a specific user. This allows the app to chart their progress and identify which parts of the app they have used.

3 Enter the name of the person who will be using the app and tap once on the **Play** button

4 Follow the instructions for games such as matching objects with each other by drawing lines between them

5 For word games, tap once on a letter to match each object correctly

Read Me Stories

This is a reading app that provides stories that can either be read by your child or automatically by the app. To use it:

1. Tap once on this icon

2. Tap once on a book to go to that series

3. Tap once on a book within a series

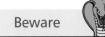

Choose a series of books!

4. Tap once on one of the buttons to select whether you want your child to listen to the book being read, or read it for themselves

5. If the book is being read by the app, the words are highlighted as it is being read so that it can be followed by your child

Beware

Narrated stories can be a good learning tool and an excellent way to keep your child occupied. However, some of the voices used for the narration can become annoying after a while.

Mathematics Apps

There are numerous mathematics apps that are not only very educational, but also a lot of fun!

MathBoard

This is one of the top mathematics apps and it can be used through a range of ages. It generates sets of quizzes, with the difficulty of the questions based on settings that are specified by the user. To use it:

1. Tap once on this icon

2. Settings are positioned on the left-hand side

3. Tap once on the **Play** button to start a quiz

< Play >

4. By default, the questions have multiple choice answers. Tap once on a answer. The results so far for the quiz are shown to the left of the current question

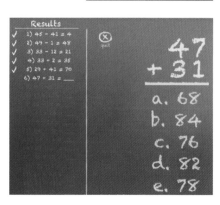

5 To the left of the questions and results is a chalkboard. This can be used to work out the current sum. Write with your finger on the chalkboard to create the sum

6 Tap once on a setting to select different options. The more options that are selected then the harder the questions in the quizzes. For instance, if more Operator Types are checked on then this will increase the types of questions that are included in the quiz

Don't forget

Student names can be added at the bottom of the Settings sections, so that different people can have their own accounts and results.

93

7 Tap once on the **Extras** Setting to access Tables and also the Problem Solver. This can be used to add specific sums and view the working for solving them

8 Tables, such as the multiplication table, can be used for general reference and revision

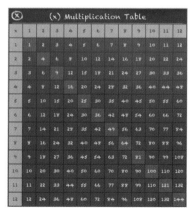

...cont'd

Beware

If the Problem Solver is used while you are in the middle of a quiz, that question will be marked as incorrect.

9 The sums become harder when more options are selected within the Settings

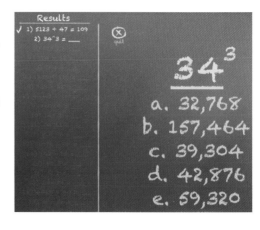

10 If a sum is too complicated, tap once on the **Show Problem** link at the bottom left-hand corner

11 The Problem Solver shows the full working for a specific sum. This is an excellent way to find out the technique for working out types of sums

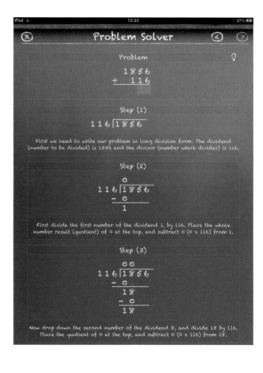

Math Bingo

This is a bingo-based game that tests adding, subtraction, multiplication and division. To use it:

1 Tap once on this icon

2 Tap once on the **Play** button

3 Tap once on an existing player or tap once on the Player button and add details for a new player

Hot tip

Math Bingo is a fun way of introducing younger children to more complex sums, particularly with the different skill levels.

4 Select the type of game you want to play. Tap once on the yellow box to use a combination

5 Select a skill level

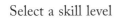

6 The questions appear at the top of the board. Tap once on an answer. When you have completed a column or a row, the word BINGO appears across it

English Apps

There are a lot of apps related to studying English as a subject, as oppposed to as a foreign language. These generally fall into three categories:

- Apps for specific exam syllabus, i.e. relevant to certain countries or examination boards

- Course study notes or companions, i.e. apps that help with set texts, such as Shakespeare and John Steinbeck

- Reference material, such as dictionaries and grammar guides

Apps for English exams

To find apps for specific exam boards:

 Enter the name of the exam board in the **App Store Search box** to find relevant apps

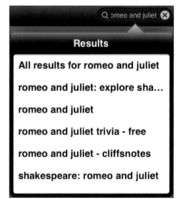

 Apps for the relevant syllabus can be reviewed and downloaded if required

Course notes

To find course study notes for relevant English texts:

1 Enter the name of the text in the **App Store Search box** to find relevant apps

2 Course study notes for the relevant text can be reviewed and downloaded if required

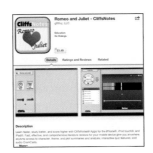

Reference material

This can be found under the Reference category in the App Store:

1 Search for the type of reference material you want to use

2 Reference items can be reviewed and downloaded if required

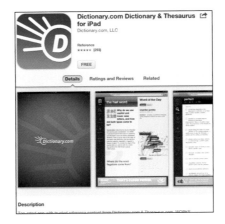

Don't forget

A lot of good dictionaries can be found in the **Reference** category. Some of the better ones usually require a fee.

Science Apps

Apps for biology, chemistry and physics generally take the form of lessons and tests in the relevant subjects, at different levels.

Finding science apps

To search for science apps, enter the name of the discipline, or a branch of it, into the App Store Search box. Relevant apps are displayed and can then be reviewed:

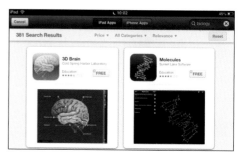

Style of science apps

Generally science apps are in the form of interactive lessons:

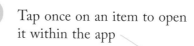 Tap once on an item to open it within the app

Don't forget

Some science apps have lessons in the form of multiple choice questions, with descriptions and explanations after each question has been answered.

2 Select a topic and tap once on the **Begin** (or **Start**) button to begin the lesson

3 The lesson is displayed, either with textual explanations, or a narration, or both

4 The lesson proceeds automatically (like a video that can be paused as you are progressing) until the topic has been completed. (In some apps the lesson may have to be advanced manually with a **Next** button to move to the next item.)

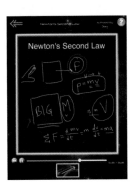

Don't forget

Some science apps have tests that can be done at the end of each section.

Science reference apps

There are several general reference apps, with one of the most useful being the periodic table of elements. Tap once on one of the elements to see its properties:

History Apps

History apps generally fall into two categories:

- This day in history apps

- Topic apps, covering specific areas of history or topics

This day in history

These are apps that contain information for what happened on a certain day in history. This includes notable events, discoveries, wars and birthdays of famous people:

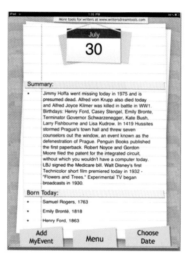

Topic apps

To find apps for specific history topics:

1 Enter the name of a historical topic in the **App Store Search box** to find relevant apps

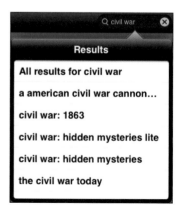

2 The app contains main topic headings for each subject

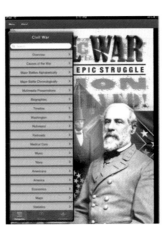

3 Within a history topic app, tap once on one of the main topic headings

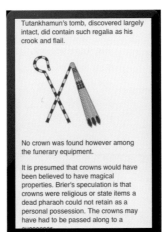

Beware

Apps that have a lot of text, such as those for history lessons, do not always have a Print function. If you want to print out the text then it has to be copied to an app that can do this, such as Pages. For details about how to do this, see Chapter Six.

4 Information about the selected topic is displayed. Swipe up and down with one finger to move through the topic

Tutankhamun's tomb, discovered largely intact, did contain such regalia as his crook and flail.

No crown was found however among the funerary equipment.

It is presumed that crowns would have been believed to have magical properties. Brier's speculation is that crowns were religious or state items a dead pharaoh could not retain as a personal possession. The crowns may have had to be passed along to a

Geography Apps

Apps for geography students generally fall into two categories:

- General geography

- Topic apps. These are apps that cover specific areas of geography such as geology or environmental geography

In addition to this, there is also a geography app that is possibly the best educational game for the iPad – Stack the Countries (see page 104).

One of the best overall geography apps is the Geography Encyclopedia. To use this:

(see page 104).

1 Tap once on this icon

2 Tap once on the main screen to move to the categories section

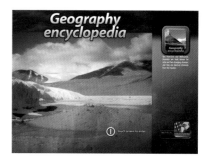

3 Main topic headings are shown on the top menu bar, with the categories for each below them. Tap once on a category to go to that topic

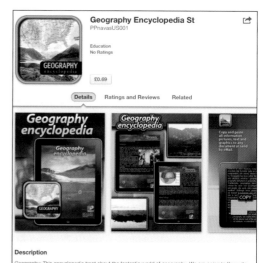

4 Information about the selected topic is displayed. Swipe up and down with one finger to move through the topic

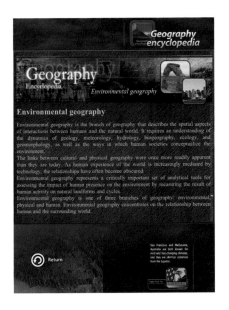

5 Each topic has text, diagrams and photos to illustrate different points and areas

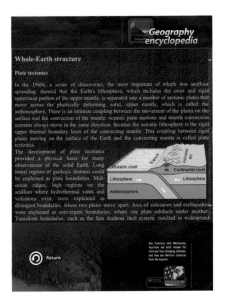

...cont'd

Stack the Countries

This is an educational game that combines multiple choice geography questions and elements of one of the best computer games of all time, Tetris. It is dangerously addictive, for children and adults alike! To use it:

1 Tap once on this icon

2 Multiple choice questions appear at the top of the screen. Tap once on an icon to select an answer

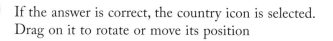

3 If the answer is correct, the country icon is selected. Drag on it to rotate or move its position

4 Tap once on the **Drop It!** button to drop the country icon onto the stand at the bottom. Build up the country icons until they reach the dotted line, at which point the game is completed and you gain a new country to study

Language Apps

Apps for learning foreign languages generally fall into two categories:

- Study apps

- Flashcards, principally for learning vocabulary

Study apps

These are apps that cover a comprehensive learning solution for foreign languages, including:

- Online tutorials

- Study notes

- Audio repetition

- Flashcards

- Text quizzes

- Audio quizzes

Don't forget

Full study apps for learning a foreign language are usually paid for apps, while flashcards are more likely to be free.

Flashcards

These are apps that deliver vocabulary details for the selected language. They can either be in the form of text cards, similar to a dictionary, or they can be audio cards where the selected words have an audio accompaniment.

Some More to Try

There are literally thousands of apps in each category of the App Store. The ones below are just a small range of some more education apps for children of different ages.

- **Color Uncovered.** An app that contains some fascinating information about color, how it works and how we interact with it. The topics contain an image with a question and then a textual explanation

- **Dragon Dictation.** This is a useful app for any children who have accessibility issues with using the iPad keyboard. It is an app that recognizes speech and converts it into text. It also has a facility for copying, pasting and deleting text that has been created

- **Flash cards by Parents Magazine.** An app containing flashcards for pre-school children. It comes with two free sets and then additional sets can be purchased. In addition to the flashcards themselves, there are also games, quizzes and tracing options

- **GoSkyWatch.** Astronomy apps are some of the most popular for the iPad. This one takes account of your own geographical location and then determines the makeup of the stars and planets when you point the iPad camera towards the sky. You can then tap on the items on the screen to find out more information about them

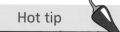

Hot tip

When searching for apps, sometimes two words are run together to create the name of the app ,e.g. GoSkyWatch.

- **iTouchiLearn.** Two apps for pre-school children, one for words and one for numbers. They provide games and activities that help with reading, writing, spelling and counting

- **iWriteWords.** Another reading and writing app for pre-school children that enables them to trace letters following a specific path on the screen

- **Math Ninja.** A mathematics app for pre-school children that allows them to adopt a Ninja character to complete multiple choice tasks in adding, subtracting, multiplication and division

- **Mental Case (Flashcards Classroom Edition).** This is another powerful flashcard app, with high quality graphics. There are pre-designed flashcards and you can also create your own, with text, audio and images

- **NASA.** This is another popular astronomy app, with a host of information and images of planets, stars and general information about NASA and space exploration

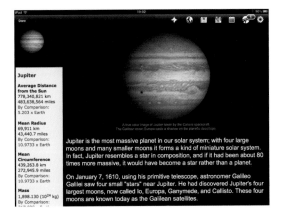

- **Pearl Diver.** An interactive mathematics app developed by educators, researchers and game developers. It takes place in a deep sea environment. It is appropriate for middle school or primary school level

- **Rocket Math.** Similar to Pearl Diver, but the games and quizzes take place in a space environment. It contains different categories that are appropriate for children of all ages and levels of ability

- **Solar Walk.** An astronomy app that enables you to explore, and learn about, the solar system in 3D

- **Solar System Journey.** An in-depth app, that explains everything about the solar system that you probably ever wanted to know

- **Stack the States.** Similar to the Stack the Countries geography app, but for the States in the USA

- **StoryKit.** An innovative writing and reading app that enables you to create your own stories. These can be based on existing books, or you can create them from scratch

- **Strip Designer.** For the artistically inclined, this is an app for creating your own cartoon strips. You can use your own photos and then add text balloons and graphics

- **TED.** This is an app that will appeal to anyone who is interested in learning and asking questions. TED stands for Technology, Entertainment and Design and the app contains a range of stimulating and challenging talks and lectures on a range of diverse subjects:

Don't forget

To view the talks on TED you need to have an active Internet connection as they are downloaded from the web when you watch them through the app.

- **Toontastic.** Another creative app, for budding animators. You can draw your own cartoons and then animate them in a game-based environment. The finished animations can also be shared with other people

6 iPad for Productivity

When it was first released, questions were asked about how effective the iPad would be in terms of productivity. However, this chapter shows how these issues have been effectively addressed by a range of apps that cover productivity, from word processing to organizational tasks such as homework apps and flashcards for revision.

Productivity on the iPad

When the iPad was first introduced the initial reaction from a lot of people was that it would be great for entertainment and communications, but how would it manage with more prosaic productivity tasks such as word processing and creating and saving documents? For parents and teachers, this is an important issue since they will want their children to use the iPad as more than just an entertainment tool. But due to the versatility of the iPad, and the wealth of productivity apps that have been developed, it can now be viewed as a genuine productivity tool. Some of the productivity possibilities that there are for the iPad are:

- Word processing

- Presentations

- Spreadsheets

- Reference material, including books and journals

- Organizational apps, such as note-taking

It's all in the apps

As with most things to do with the iPad it is the apps that make productivity possible. There is a productivity category within the App Store where there are a range of apps for creating, and viewing, content.

Don't forget

Generally, productivity apps save your work as you create it so you do not have to keep remembering to constantly select Save.

The built-in Newsstand app can also be used to store books and magazines which can be used for productivity purposes.

Saving Your Work

For anyone who has grown up with computers and is used to a clear file structure, the first question when faced with an iPad is sometimes, 'Where do I save things?'. Unlike a Windows PC with Windows Explorer, or a Mac with the Finder, there is no obvious place to save files or create folders for content. This is because there isn't one. So where do you save your essays, presentations or photos once they have been created?

Self-contained saving

Instead of having a separate structure into which you can save files, content is saved within the apps in which they are created. So, if you write an essay with the Pages word processing app, this is where it will be saved, and similarly if you create a presentation within the Keynote app. Documents can be viewed as follows:

1   Tap once on the **Documents** button

2   All saved documents can be viewed here

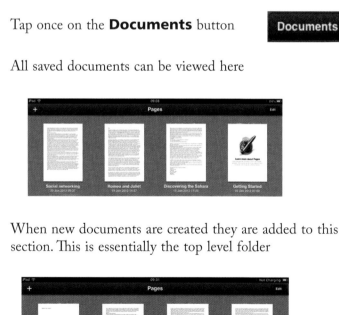

3   When new documents are created they are added to this section. This is essentially the top level folder

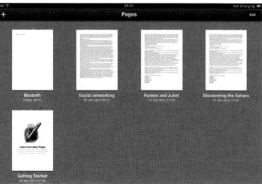

Don't forget

The button in Step 1 will usually be relevant to the type of app, e.g. for the Keynote presentation app, the button is Presentations, but the process is the same.

Hot tip

A lot of apps from Apple are linked to iCloud so your work can be stored and shared here.

Adding folders

Despite the lack of a folder structure within the iPad operating system, folders can be created within some productivity apps, such as Pages. To do this:

1 Tap and hold on a document until it starts to jiggle. Drag it over another document icon

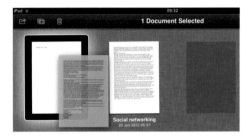

2 The new folder is created. Tap once here to give it a relevant name, then tap anywhere outside the folder to finish, or tap once on **Done** on the keyboard

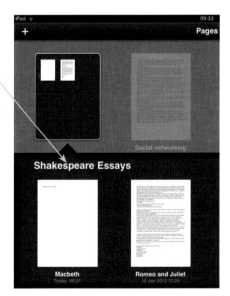

Beware

You cannot create sub-folders, i.e. folders within folders. So the folder structure can only go down one level.

3 The new folder appears in the main document area next to existing files

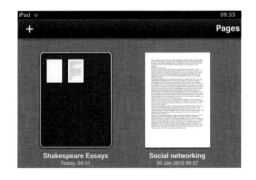

Printing Your Work

Printing from an iPad has advantages and disadvantages. The advantage is that it is done wirelessly so you do not have to worry about connecting wires and cables to a printer. The disadvantage is that there's a limited number of printers that work with the iPad printing system, although this number is going up all the time.

AirPrint

Content from an iPad is printed using the AirPrint system that is part of the iOS operating system. This is a wireless printing system that connects to your printer through your Wi-Fi network. However, not all printers are AirPrint-enabled so it may not work with your current printer.

AirPrint can print content from Safari, Mail, Photos, Pages, Keynote, Numbers and PDF documents in iBooks. Some third-party apps have AirPrint facilities but this depends on individual developers. To print items using AirPrint:

Don't forget

Check on the Apple website for a list of AirPrint-enabled printers.

1. Tap once on the tools option and select one of the Print options

2. Tap once on the **Print** link

Beware

Some developers offer third-party printing apps for the iPad. However, these work with varying degrees of success.

3. Select a printer or, if it has already been set up, tap once on the **Print** button to print

4. If your printer is not AirPrint compatible this will be shown in the Printer dialog box

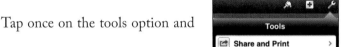
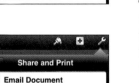

Pages

Pages is a word processing app for the iPad and also other Mac computers and mobile devices. It is created by Apple and is part of the iWork suite of apps that also includes Keynote for presentations and Numbers for spreadsheets.

Pages is a powerful word processor for a mobile device and although it does not have the same range of features as the version for desktop or laptop computers, it is more than capable of producing high quality documents.

Creating documents

Once you have downloaded the Pages app, documents can be created as follows:

 Tap once on this icon

 Tap once on this button to create a new document

Tap once on the **Create Document** button

Pages comes with a range of pre-designed templates that can be used as the basis of your document. Tap once on a template to select it for your document. All elements of a template can be replaced with your own content

5 The document is created, based on the selected template. (If the Blank template is selected, there will be no content in the document)

6 Tap once on the **Documents** button to view the document in the Pages folder environment

7 The document appears here in the folder area

8 Tap once on the file name and type a new name as required and tap once on the **Done** button

...cont'd

Formatting text

Once a new document has been created, content can be added to it. To do this:

1 Tap once on the new document and use the keyboard to add text. Tap once on these buttons to format selected text

2 Tap once on these buttons to, from left to right, change the font, decrease the font size, set a specific font size and increase the font size

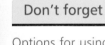

3 Tap once on these buttons to, from left to right, create bold, italic or underlined text or set the text alignment

Selecting text

In order to perform the formatting on the previous page, text has to first be selected. Text also has to be selected if you want to copy and paste it.

1 To change the insertion point, tap and hold until the magnifying glass appears

2 Drag the magnifying glass to move the insertion point

3 Tap once at the insertion point to access the selection buttons

4 Double-tap on a word to select it. Tap once on **Cut** or **Copy** as required

5 Drag the selection handles to expand or contract the selection

6 If text has been copied, tap and hold at a new point on the page and tap once on **Paste**

...cont'd

Adding media

With Pages you can add a variety of different types of content, in addition to text. One of the most commonly-used types of media in word processing documents are images. To add these in Pages:

1 Tap once here and tap once on the Media button. Tap once on a location on your iPad from which to select an image. Navigate to this and tap once on an image to add it to the document

Hot tip

Images can be incorporated with text in different ways using the **Wrap** option. The options are **Automatic**, **Around** and, **Above and Below**. There is also a button that can be dragged to **On** so that the image moves with the text.

2 Tap once on an image to select it. Drag the placeholder buttons to resize the image

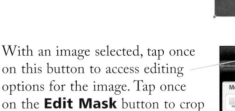

3 With an image selected, tap once on this button to access editing options for the image. Tap once on the **Edit Mask** button to crop the image

Hot tip

The Mask option can also be accessed by double-tapping on an image in a document.

4 Drag the resizing handles to select the area you want to keep. Tap once on the **Mask** button to finish the operation

Other elements that can be added within Pages are:

1 Tap once on the same button as for images and tap once on the **Tables** button to add pre-designed tables. Tap once on a table to add it to a document. Tap once to select it in a document and resize it in the same way as an image

2 Tap once on the **Charts** button to add pre-designed charts. Tap once on a chart to add it to a document. Tap once to select it in a document. Once it is selected, tap once on **Edit Data,** (above the chart) to add your own data

Hot tip

To move through the pages of the Tables, Charts and Shapes sections, tap once on the small dots at the bottom of the window.

3 Tap once on the **Shapes** button to add pre-designed shapes. Tap once on a shape to add it to a document. Tap once to select it in a document and resize it in the same way as an image

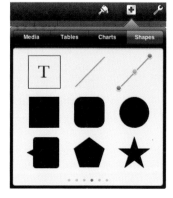

...cont'd

Tools and Settings

To access additional tools and settings options:

1 Tap once on this button on the toolbar

2 The available tools are for Share and Print, Find (for finding items in a document), Document Setup, Settings and general Help information

3 Tap once on the **Share and Print** link to access options for this. There are various options for sharing, including emailing and sharing to the online iWork.com facility

4 Tap once on the **Settings** link to access options for this. This includes activating the spell checker and the word count and also options for setting guidelines on a page

Keynote

Keynote is another app in Apple's iWork suite. It is used for creating presentations, in a similar style to the Microsoft PowerPoint program. It can be used to make individual slides and also slideshow presentations with multiple slides.

Creating presentations

To create presentations in Keynote:

 Tap once on this icon

Don't forget

Keynote is an excellent app for school projects and also for giving talks to classmates.

Tap once on this button to create a new presentation

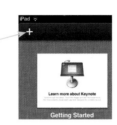

Tap once on the **Create Presentation** button

Tap once on a template to select it for the first slide of your presentation

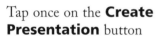

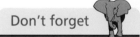
Don't forget

New presentations are stored in the same way as with Pages documents and folders can also be created in the same way.

The content of the template forms the basis for the first slide of your presentation. This can now be edited with your own content

...cont'd

Adding content

The main elements of slides in Keynote are images and text. These can be added by editing the existing content that is provided by the template. To do this:

 Tap once on an image to select it and tap once on this icon on the image or on the toolbar

2. Select a new image in the same way as for Pages. If an image is already selected in the slide it will be replaced by the new one. If nothing is selected the image will be inserted

3. Tap once here and tap once on the **Style** button to select styles for the appearance of the image

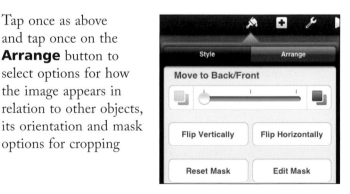

4. Tap once as above and tap once on the **Arrange** button to select options for how the image appears in relation to other objects, its orientation and mask options for cropping

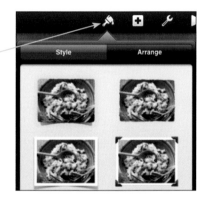

To add and format text:

1 Double-tap on the placeholder text to add your own

2 Enter text with the keyboard

3 Resize the text by dragging the resizing handles or hold and drag to move the whole text box

...cont'd

4 Tap once here and tap on the **Style** button to select a style for the selected text. This includes drop shadows and a colored background behind the text. Tap once on the **Style Options** link to access more options

5 Select a color for the text. Tap once on the **Border** and **Effects** buttons to access more options

6 Tap once as above and tap on the **Text** button to select formatting options and also pre-designed styles that can be applied to the text box

Don't forget

Drag the **Move to Back/Front** button to change the order of a text box in relation to other objects, such as images.

7 Tap once as above and tap on the **Arrange** button to select options for how the text appears in relation to other objects and alignment options

Adding slides

Once you have created your first slide you can then add more to build up your presentation. To do this:

1 Tap once here and select a new style for the subsequent slide. This can either be the same as the first slide or it can be a new style. Tap once on a slide to add it to the presentation

125

2 The new slide is shown in the presentation here. Enter content in the same way as for the first slide

...cont'd

Animations and Transitions

One of the most eye-catching features of presentation apps is their ability to apply animated effects to objects and slides. Animations can be applied to images or text within individual slides. This determines how they are introduced and removed from the slide. To do this:

1 Tap once on this button on the toolbar to access the animation options

2 Tap once on an item in a slide to select it. This activates the Build In and Build Out buttons

Beware

Do not use too many Build In and Build Out effects. Otherwise the slide may become too 'busy' and distracting for the viewer.

3 Tap once for the **Build In** option. This determines how the object is animated into the slide. Repeat the process for the **Build Out** effect, if required

4 When animations have been added this is denoted on the object by these icons

5 In the Build In or Build Out window, tap once on the **Order** button at the bottom and drag here to change the order of the animated effects for each object on the slide

Beware

Keep objects together if you are reordering them, i.e. do not split up an image and a text box.

To create transition effects between slides:

① Tap once on this button on the toolbar to access the transition options

② Tap once on one of the slides in the left-hand panel. Tap once here to add a transition

③ Tap once on a transition effect

④ Tap once on a slide to view the transition effect that has been applied to it

⑤ Tap once on this button on the toolbar to preview the slideshow. This can be done at any point during the creation of the presentation

Numbers

Numbers is the spreadsheet app in the iWork suite. It is used for creating spreadsheets containing plain text and also formula with tables of figures.

Creating spreadsheets

To create spreadsheets in Numbers:

1. Tap once on this icon

2. Tap once on this button to create a new spreadsheet

3. Tap once on the **Create Spreadsheet** button

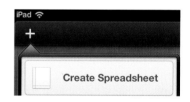

4. Tap once on a template to select it for the spreadsheet. If you want to create your own spreadsheet from scratch, tap once on the Blank template

5. The spreadsheet is saved into the folder area in the same way as with Pages documents and Keynote presentations

Adding content

Content can be added to cells of a spreadsheet in Numbers in different formats. These are:

- Numbers
- Date
- Text
- Formulae

To add content:

1 Double-tap on a cell to access the input options

2 Tap once here to enter numbers with the keypad

3 Tap once here to add a date or duration format, using the buttons to the right. Use the keypad to enter a specific day

4 Tap once here to enter text with the keypad

Don't forget

Tap once on a cell to select it, rather than double-tapping for the input options. Once it is selected, formatting options can be applied.

Don't forget

Tap once on the **Done** button once you have input the required items.

Adding formulae

The ability to add formulae to cells is a vital part of the functionality of a spreadsheet app as it enables the app to perform calculations with the data that has been added. To do this:

130

1 Tap once here to enter a formula for a cell

2 Tap once on the **Functions** button to access the different available types of formulae. Tap once on one to select it

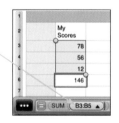

3 Tap once on a cell and drag over consecutive cells to add them to the formula as a group. This is added next to the selected formula

4 Tap once on individual cells to add them to the formula as individual items.
This can be used to add non-consecutive items, if required

5 Tap once on the green button to accept a formula and the red button to reject it

Formatting content

Content within individual cells of a spreadsheet can be formatted, as can the spreadsheet as a whole. To do this:

  Tap once on a cell to select it

Tap once here and tap once on the **Table** button. Tap once on a formatting option for the style of the spreadsheet

Tap once on the **Table Options** button to access more formatting options for the table

Tap once on the **Headers** button to select options for the spreadsheet's headers and footers

Don't forget

Table options can be set for the table name, showing or hiding the table border, different shades for alternating rows, options for formatting the table grid and font options that apply to all text within the table.

...cont'd

5 Tap once on the **Cells** button to select formatting options for the selected cell

Within the **Cells** section, tap once on the **Text Options** link to access options for editing the size, color and font of the text in a selected cell.

6 Tap once on the **Format** button to select formatting options for the content of the selected cell, e.g. to show figures as numbers, currency or percentages. Each option has additional settings to refine the selection, e.g. adding decimal places for numbers

7 Tap once here to add content in the same way as for Pages and Keynote, i.e. photos, tables, charts and shapes

Hot tip

Under the **Share** option, a spreadsheet can be emailed in a Numbers, PDF or Excel format.

8 Tap once here to share and print the spreadsheet, find items in the spreadsheet, access Numbers settings and general Help

Adding and editing sheets

Within a spreadsheet it is possible to add sheets, move the sheet on which you are working, resize it and edit the size of rows and columns. To do this:

 Tap once here to add a new sheet

2 Tap once on a cell to select it and drag on this button to move the spreadsheet

Hot tip

Cells can be expanded by dragging to accommodate text. Text can also be wrapped in a cell by selecting the **Wrap Text in Cell** option within the **Cells** section.

3 Drag on this button to resize the spreadsheet

4 Tap once on a cell to select it and then tap here to select a column (or row if selected vertically). Drag to resize the selected item

Hot tip

When a column is selected there are options for deleting it, inserting another column and sorting the content of the column according to ascending or descending values.

133

iBooks

iBooks is an app that enables you to access, download and read books and educational textbooks. It has a similar interface to the App Store and the iTunes Store, so it should be familiar to anyone who has used these. The iBooks app can initially be downloaded from within the App Store. To do this:

1 Access the iBooks app in the App Store and tap once here to download it

2 Tap once on this icon once the **iBooks** app has been downloaded

3 The iBooks app interface consists of a bookcase, which is empty initially. Tap once on the **Store** button to access the iBooks store

4 Navigate through the iBooks Store in the same way as the App Store to find the required titles

5 Use these buttons to search for items within the iBooks Store

Downloading books

Once you have identified appropriate books they can then be downloaded to the iBooks bookcase. To do this:

1 Tap once on the book name or title to view its details

2 Review the details of the book and view sample pages. Tap once here to download the book

Don't forget

The iBooks bookcase is also known as the Library. Use these buttons at the top right-hand side of the toolbar to view the content by icon or text. Tap once on the **Edit** button to delete an item, by tapping on it once and then tapping once on the **Delete** button.

135

3 Downloaded books appear on the iBooks bookcase. Tap once on a book cover to open it

...cont'd

Reading an iBook

Once you have opened an iBook:

1 Tap once on a page in an iBook to access the top toolbar

2 Tap once on these buttons to, from left to right, change the brightness, search for items or bookmark a page

3 Tap once on this button to view the Table of Contents and the Glossary (if there is one)

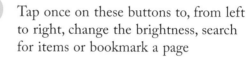

4 Tap once on this button to access a page where you can enter your own notes

5 Tap once here to add your own notes or to highlight a piece of text

Finding textbooks

Within iBooks there is a range of textbooks that can be used for schoolwork. To find these:

 Enter the relevant keywords in the **iBooks Store Search box,** based on the subject of the textbook

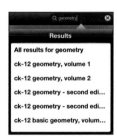

Tap once on a title to review its contents. Tap once on the **Free** button to download it

Navigate through the book contents by tapping once to access the main toolbar. Swipe left or right to move between pages

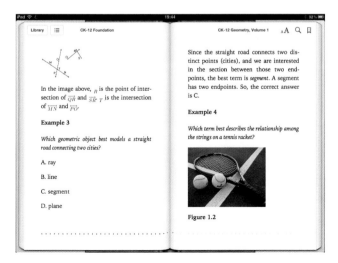

Newsstand

Newsstand is a built-in iPad app that is similar to iBooks, except that it deals with magazines, newspapers and journals rather than books. To use Newsstand:

 Tap once on this icon

 The Newsstand bookcase is initially empty. Tap once on the Store button to access the Newsstand store

Don't forget

For a lot of items within the Newsstand it is free to download a sample version but you then need to pay a subscription for the selected newspaper, journal or magazine.

 The Newsstand Store is incorporated within the App Store. Items can be found in the same way as with other items in the App Store

4 When you have found a suitable magazine, newspaper or journal, review and download it in the same way as with an app or an iBook

5 Downloaded items appear on the Newsstand bookcase (Library). Tap once on a cover to open that publication

139

6 Tap once on a page to access the top toolbar. This contains items for accessing the homepage of the publication, a contents page and options for zooming and sharing a page via email, Facebook or to a Photo Album

iTunes U

For older students, and also adults interested in further education, the iTunes U app provides access to a wide range of courses from universities and schools around the world. This is a fantastic resource, made all the better by the fact that the majority of courses are free. To use iTunes U:

 Access the iTunes U app in the App Store and download it

 Tap once on the **Catalog** button to access the iTunes U catalog of courses

The courses within iTunes U can be accessed from the homepage

Tap once on the **Universities & Colleges** button and tap once on an establishment from which you would like to view their range of courses

Don't forget

Different establishments have their own style for presenting their material.

5 Navigate from the home page of the selected establishment to find their courses

6 Tap once on the **Subscribe** button to download the course material

Don't forget

If there is supplementary material for the course, this will be shown by a blue circle at the top right-hand corner of the course cover on the iTunes U bookcase.

7 The selected course is downloaded to the iTunes U bookcase. Tap once on a cover to access the course content

8 Swipe through the pages to view the course content and use the tabs down the right-hand side to view additional items such as notes pages and further information

Keeping Organized

Parents and teachers always want their children and pupils to try to be as organized as possible when approaching their school work. With the iPad this can now all be done digitally rather than having to rely on hard copy diaries and timetables. There are various types of apps that can help with this:

- Homework apps. These are apps that act in a similar way to a traditional school timetable. Classes and items of homework can be added to act as a mobile reminder about school work and activities

- General organization such as note taking apps, calendars and address books

- Flashcard apps. These are apps for creating your own reminders for revision for specific subjects

MyHomework

This is representative of homework apps. To use this:

142

1   Tap once on this icon

2   Tap once on this button to show and hide the main toolbar on any page to return to the home screen

3   Tap once on these icons to return to the home screen, access the homework calendar, add new homework items or view information that has been added by teachers

4 Tap once on the plus sign next to **Classes**

Classes   +

5 Tap once on **Add a Class Manually** button

Add a Class Manually

6 Enter the subjects and times for the required school classes. Tap once on the **Save** button to create the classes

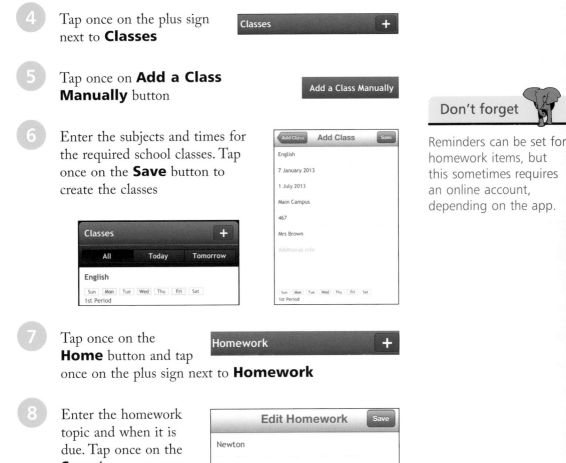

Classes	+
All	Today	Tomorrow

English
Sun Mon Tue Wed Thu Fri Sat
1st Period

Add Class — **Add Class** — Save

English
7 January 2013
1 July 2013
Main Campus
467
Mrs Brown
Additional Info

Sun Mon Tue Wed Thu Fri Sat
1st Period

7 Tap once on the **Home** button and tap once on the plus sign next to **Homework**

Homework   +

8 Enter the homework topic and when it is due. Tap once on the **Save** button to create the homework item

Edit Homework	Save
Newton	
Physics	
Study	
15 February 2013	
10:30	
Medium	

9 The item is added to the Homework section

Homework	+
All	Class	Priority	Type

All

Newton	Fri 15 Feb
Physics	Study

...cont'd

Evernote

This is one of the most popular note-taking apps. It is available on the iPad and there are also versions for the iPhone and desktop PCs and laptops (for both Mac OS X and Windows). This means that whatever you add to Evernote, it will be synchronized and available over all of your devices. Notes in Evernote on the iPad can be created with text, audio and photos. To use Evernote:

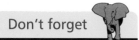

Don't forget

Once you have created an Evernote account you can use the login details to view your Evernote account on any mobile device or computer with Internet access.

144

1. Tap once on this icon

2. Tap once on the **Create Account** button. This enables you to create your Evernote account so that you can access your information from different sources. This is free. When you have an account, tap once on the **Sign In** button

3. The home screen displays folder tabs for storing all of your Evernote content. Tap once on the **All Notes** heading to view your notes

4 To create a new note, tap once on this button

5 Enter details for the new note. Use the buttons at the top to add audio and photos to the note and also take a photo with the iPad for the note. Tap once on the **Done** button once you have finished the note, then tap once on the **Close** button

6 The note appears in the **All Notes** area. Tap once on it to edit it

7 Tap once here to minimize a folder tab and return to the home screen

8 On the home screen use these quick link buttons to, from top to bottom, create a new note, take a photo, or create digital notes from hard copy documents

Calendars

The iPad has a built-in Calendar app that can be used to note appointments for social events and also school work. To use the Calendar app:

1 Tap once on this icon

2 Use these buttons to view the calendar in different formats

3 Tap once on a date, or

4 Tap once on the **Today** button in the bottom left-hand corner to view the calendar for the current date

5 Tap and hold on a time slot to add a new event

6 Enter details of the event and tap once on the **Done** button

Address Books

Children usually have a lot of friends and contacts so it is useful to have somewhere where their details can be recorded and saved. For parents this can also be useful if they need to get in touch with their child's friends. On the iPad the Contacts app serves as an address book. To use this:

1 Tap once on this icon

2 Tap once on this button to add a new contact

3 Enter the details for the new contact

4 Tap once on the **Done** button

5 The contact is added to the address book. Use these buttons to contact them via text or video messaging or share their details with someone else or add them to your favorite contacts

6 Select a contact and tap once on the **Edit** button to edit their details

Don't forget

Your contacts can be used in a selection of apps, including Mail, Game Center, FaceTime and Messages.

147

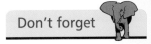

Don't forget

There is also a built-in Reminders app that can be used to create specific reminders, which can be set to appear in the Notification Center.

Flashcards

Flashcards are revision aids that come with information already inserted on them and you can also make up your own flashcards for specific subjects. Flashcard apps are similar in their functionality. The examples here are for the Flashcards app:

1. Tap once on this icon

2. On the home screen, tap once on the **add deck** button, in the bottom right-hand corner

3. Tap once on the **Search Decks** button and select a source location

4. Tap once on one of the main categories. Navigate to a topic and tap once on it to view the flashcard content

5. The content (questions and answers) is displayed

6. If you want to use these flashcards, tap once on the **Download** button

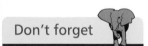

Don't forget

The content for the flashcards is essentially a database of information. Once it is downloaded it is converted into the flashcard format.

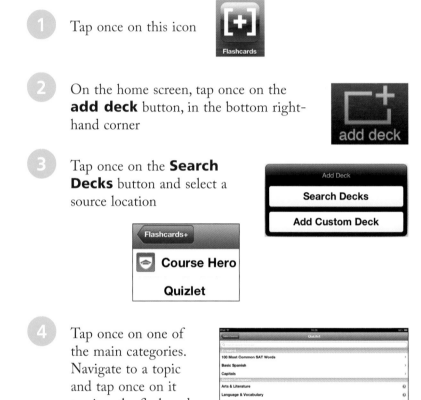

7 This will download the content to a deck of flashcards within the **Decks** area. Tap once on a deck name to access the relevant flashcards

iPad 🛜	16:32
ⓘ	**Flashcards+**

Decks

Botany Ch.10 (Emily Rousseau)

8 The question is displayed on the front of the flashcard

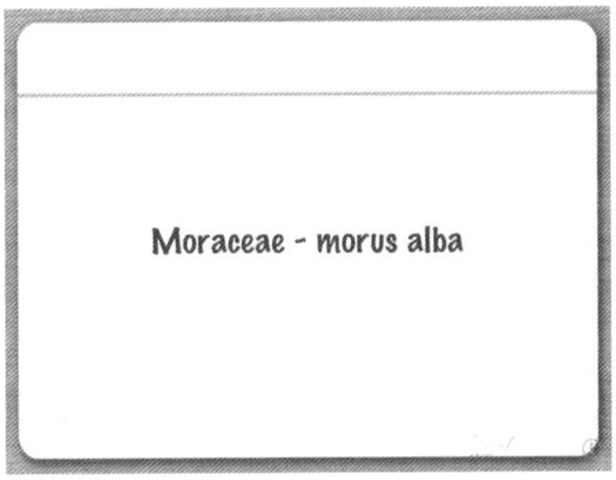

Moraceae - morus alba

9 Swipe left or right to view the answer on the reverse of the flashcard

White Mulberry

Beware

Although you can edit the pre-designed flashcards, make sure that you do not change anything that makes them incorrect.

10 Tap once on the tick to move to the next flashcard. Tap once on **edit card** to change the card

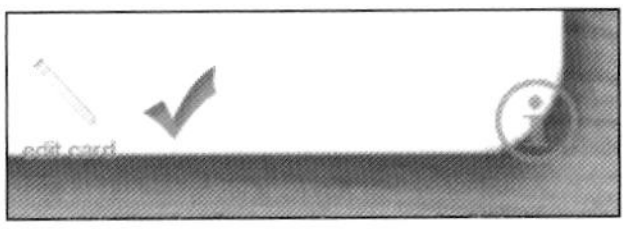

edit card ✓

11 Tap on the screen and tap once on the button in the top left-hand corner to go back up to the top level of the deck of flashcards

Biology

149

...cont'd

Creating your own flashcards

In addition to the pre-designed flashcards it is also possible to create decks of your own flashcards. To do this:

1 On the home screen, tap once on the **add deck** button and tap once on the **Add Custom Deck** button

2 Enter a Deck Name, Deck Subject and Deck Description. Tap once on the **Save** button

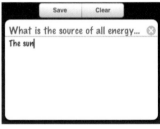

3 Enter the question above the red line and the answer below it. Tap once on the **Save** button

4 On the home screen tap once on the deck name under the **Decks** heading

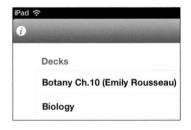

5 Tap once on a deck to view its flashcards

7 Photos and Videos

With the proliferation of mobile devices such as the iPad, it has never been easier for children to create and share photos and videos. This chapter shows how to use the Photos app for working with images and the iMovie app for editing video. It also shows how to view videos on the iPad.

Capturing Photos

Because of their mobility and the quality of the screen, iPads are excellent for displaying photos. Photos can be captured directly with the iPad using one of the two built-in cameras (one on the front and one on the back) and then viewed, edited and shared using the Photos app. To do this:

Beware

When using the cameras, particularly the one on the back, make sure that you do not put your fingers over them. This is more likely to occur when you rotate the iPad during use.

Hot tip

Screenshot images can also be captured on the iPad. These are images of what is on the screen at the time. To capture a screenshot, hold down the **On/Off button** and press the **Home button**. The image will be saved within the Photos app.

1 Tap once on the **Camera** app

2 Tap once on this button to capture a photo

3 Tap once on this button to swap between the front or back cameras on the iPad

4 Tap once on the **Options** button

5 Drag the **Grid** button to **On** to place a grid over the screen, if required. This can make it easier to frame photos

Viewing Photos

Once photos have been captured they can be viewed and organized in the Photos app. To do this:

 Tap once on the **Photos** app

 All photos, and videos, that have been taken are shown here, under the **Photos** section

 Tap once on a photo to view it at full-screen size

Hot tip

If the toolbars on a full-screen size photo disappear, tap once on the photo to make them visible again.

Don't forget

Swipe left and right to move between full-screen size photos.

 Tap once with one finger or drag here to move through all of the available photos

 Tap once with two fingers to return the photo to its thumbnail size, or tap once on the **Photos** button

Creating Slideshows

Photos can also be viewed in a slideshow format in the Photos app. To do this:

 Tap once on the **Slideshow** button, either in the Photos section or when a photo is being viewed at full-screen size

Slideshow

2 Tap once here to select a transition between photos

3 Tap once on one of the transition effects to add it to the slideshow. This will be applied when one photo moves to another

4 Drag this button to **On** and tap once on the **Music** link to select music for the slideshow

5 Tap once on the **Start Slideshow** button

Creating Albums

Within the Photo app it is possible to create different albums into which you can store photos. To do this:

1. Tap once on the **Albums** button

2. Tap once on this button to create a new album

3. Enter a name for the new album

4. Tap once on the **Save** button

5. Tap once on each photo you want to add to the album or tap once on the **Select All Photos** button to add all of the photos to the new album

6. Tap once on the **Done** button

Don't forget

If photos have been set up to be shared via the online iCloud service, they will appear under the Photo Stream button. This means they will appear automatically on any of your other iCloud-enabled devices. Photo Stream can be turned on in the **Settings** app, under either **iCloud** or **Photos & Camera**.

Beware

When photos are placed in an album they remain in the main Photos section. However, if they are deleted from the Photos section they will be removed from any albums into which they have been placed too.

...cont'd

 The new album is created

 Tap once on an album to view its contents

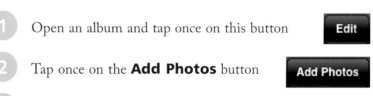

Adding photos to an album

New photos can be added to an album at any time. To do this:

156

1 Open an album and tap once on this button   Edit

2 Tap once on the **Add Photos** button   Add Photos

3 Select the photos you want to add in the same way as selecting them for a new album, by tapping once

 Tap once on the **Done** button

Editing Photos

The Photos app has some options to perform some basic photo editing operations. To use this:

1 Open a photo at full-screen size and tap once on the **Edit** button

2 Tap once on the **Rotate** button to rotate the photo 90 degrees at a time. Tap once on the **Enhance** button to have auto-color enhancements applied. Tap once on the **Red-Eye** button and tap on any red-eye in a photo

3 Tap once on the **Crop** button to access a grid with which you can crop a photo. Drag on the corners of the grid to create the required area you want to keep for the photo

4 Tap once on the **Crop** button to apply the cropped area in the photo

5 Tap once on the **Save** button to keep any editing actions that have been performed

Sharing Photos

Within the Photos app there are a number of ways to share and use photos. To do this:

Hot tip

Photos can be attached directly to an email in the Mail app, by pressing and holding in the body of the email and tapping once on the **Insert Photo or Video** button. A photo can then be selected from the Photos app.

1 In the Photos section tap once on this button

2 Tap once on a photo (or photos) to select it and tap once on the Share button. Tap once on either the Mail, Twitter, Facebook or Print option. (For Twitter and Facebook you will need the appropriate accounts, see Chapter Nine for details)

3 Photos can also be shared when they are being viewed at full-screen size. Tap once on the same button as in Step 1 and select one of the options

Hot tip

Use the **Assign to Contact** option in Step 2 to set a photo for contacts in your address book (Contacts).

4 If you select to email a photo it will be inserted automatically into a new email message, ready to send

Creative Photo Effects

As well as editing and sharing photos there are a number of fun creative effects that can be achieved. This is done with the Photo Booth app. To do this:

 Tap once on this icon

The different special effects are shown through the camera. Tap once to select the desired effect

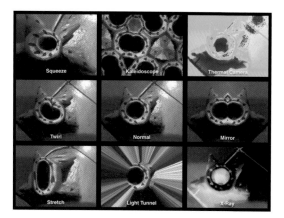

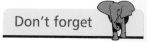

Don't forget

Children enjoy using the effects in the Photo Booth app and they are sometimes more creative at using it than adults.

Review the image and capture it in the same way as for any other photo

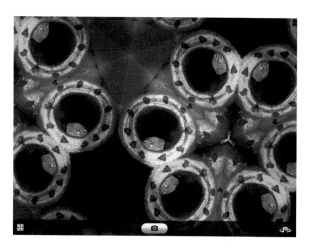

Capturing Video

Video can also be captured on an iPad and this too is done with one of the built-in cameras. To capture video:

 Tap once on the **Camera** app

 Drag this button to the right to activate the video function

 Tap once on this button to start recording video. Tap on it again to stop recording

Recorded video is saved in the **Photos** section of the Photos app

 Tap once on a video thumbnail and tap here to play it

Editing Video

Once video has been captured it can then be edited to produce a more stylish final product. This cannot be done with any of the built-in iPad apps but there are video editing apps that can be downloaded from the App Store. The most popular is Apple's own iMovie. To use this:

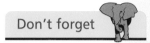

 Tap once on this icon

Within the iMovie interface tap once here to start a new video project

Tap once on this button to view videos that have already been captured. These appear as video clips in the area above the video button

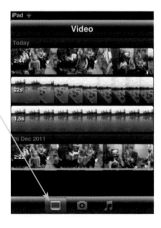

Tap once on a video clip and tap once on the blue arrow to add it to the video project

...cont'd

5 The clip is placed on the timeline. This is the basis for the video project

6 Tap once here to preview the video clip on the timeline. This previews everything that is placed here

To split a video clip, tap on it once to select it. Then drag the clip so that the pink playhead is at the position where you want to split it. Then swipe downwards over the playhead. Once a clip has been split the two new clips can be edited separately. They can also be reordered by dragging them in front of, or behind, each other.

7 Tap once on a video clip to select it. Drag here to trim the video clip. This appears at the beginning and the end of the clip

8 Swipe left and right to move through the timeline

9 Tap once here to select photos to add to the timeline. Browse to them via these locations on your iPad

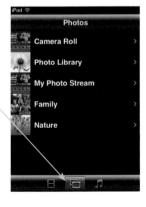

Adding audio and transitions

Audio effects can be added to video projects, as can transitions between video clips. To do this:

1 Tap once here to select audio to add to the timeline. Tap once on a link to select audio from that location

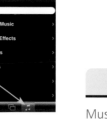

Beware

Music that you have downloaded from iTunes will not usually be available to use in an iMovie video due to copyright laws.

2 The selected audio clip is added to the timeline, underneath the video clip

3 Tap once on an audio clip and drag on the orange markers to trim it in the same way as with a video clip

4 Tap once here to view the audio timeline for the video clip

Don't forget

When you create a voiceover recording there is a 3, 2, 1 countdown between when you tap on the Record button and start recording.

5 Tap once here and tap once on the **Record** button to record a voiceover for the video

6 The voiceover is placed on the timeline and can be selected and moved in the same way as a video clip

7 Add a new video clip to the timeline. Tap once here to edit the transition effect between clips

8 Tap once on a transition effect to add that between two video clips

Don't forget

If a video clip has been split it will have a blank transition between the two clips. A new transition can be added in the same way as for editing an existing one.

9 Tap once here to place the beginning of one clip underneath the end of the previous one. This ensures a smoother transition

Adding titles

Textual titles can be added to video clips on the timeline, such as for opening and closing credits. To do this:

Hot tip

Titles appear over the length of a clip. If you want to create opening and closing titles, split the video clips at the beginning and end of the project. Or, capture some video of a black screen, or use a black, or colored, photo and then place the titles over this.

1 Double-tap on a clip to access the **Clip Settings** window. Tap once on the **Title Style** link

2 Tap once on a style to select it

3 Type the title in the text box on the video clip

Working with Video Projects

Once a video project has been completed it can be managed on the iMovie home screen. To do this:

 Tap once on the this button once a video project has been completed

2 All video projects are displayed here

3 Tap once on the title and type a new one, as required

4 As new projects are created they are added next to the first one

...cont'd

5 Swipe left and right to select projects. If you tap on them, they will open for editing

6 Select a project and tap once here and tap once on **Delete Project** to remove it

7 Tap once on this button to create a new project

8 Select a project and tap once on this button to play it

9 Select a project and tap once on this button to upload it to iTunes

10 Select a project and tap once on this button to share it to a variety of locations

Watching Videos

As the name suggests, the Videos app can be used to download and view video content. To do this:

1 Tap once on this icon

2 The Videos app is initially empty of content. Tap once here to access video content in the iTunes Store

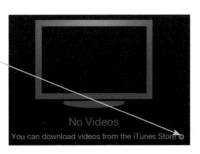

3 Search for videos using either the default Featured screen or tap once on the Top Charts or Genius buttons for more suggestions. Type keywords into the **Search box** to look for specific items

4 Use these buttons to move between film and TV content

Beware

Videos can take up a lot of storage space once they are downloaded to your iPad and you may quickly find that you have used up all of your storage if you are downloading a lot of video files.

Don't forget

If you rent videos from the iTunes Store you have to watch them within 30 days. Once you have started watching the video you have to finish watching it within 48 hours. Once the rental period has expired, the video is deleted from your iPad.

...cont'd

 Tap once on an item to review its content. Tap once here to download it. This is usually in the form of buying or renting a video

6 The video starts to download to the Videos app

7 When the video has downloaded, it appears in the Videos app. Tap once on the cover to view its contents

8 Tap once here to play a video

8 Music, Games and More

For entertainment the iPad is hard to beat. Games and music are the staple of many children and this chapter shows how they can make the most of them.

Using iTunes

Music on the iPad can be downloaded and played using the iTunes and the Music apps respectively. iTunes links to the iTunes Store, from where music, and other content, can be bought and downloaded to your iPad. To do this:

1 Tap once on this icon

2 Tap once on the **Music** button on the iTunes toolbar at the bottom of the window

3 Use these buttons at the top of the window to find music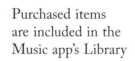

4 Tap once on an item to view it. Tap once here to buy an album or tap on the button next to a song to buy that individual song

5 Purchased items are included in the Music app's Library

Playing Music

Once music has been bought on iTunes it can be played on your iPad using the Music app. To do this:

1 Tap once on this icon

2 Use these buttons to find songs by different criteria

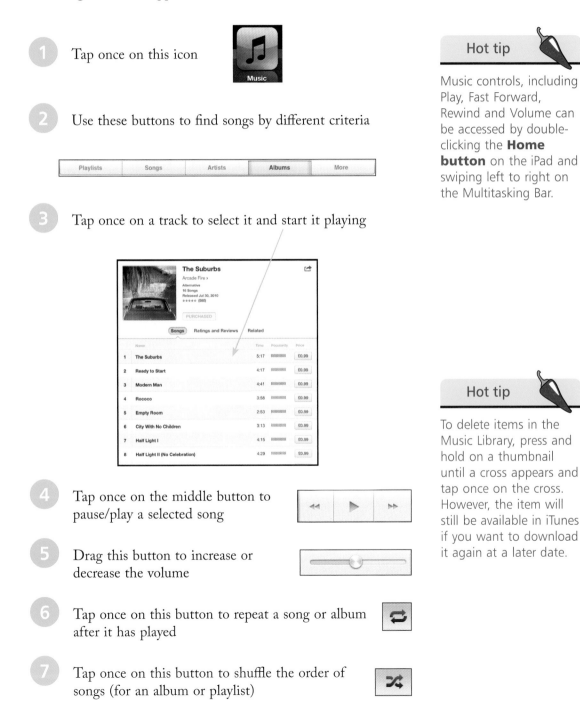

3 Tap once on a track to select it and start it playing

4 Tap once on the middle button to pause/play a selected song

5 Drag this button to increase or decrease the volume

6 Tap once on this button to repeat a song or album after it has played

7 Tap once on this button to shuffle the order of songs (for an album or playlist)

Hot tip

Music controls, including Play, Fast Forward, Rewind and Volume can be accessed by double-clicking the **Home button** on the iPad and swiping left to right on the Multitasking Bar.

Hot tip

To delete items in the Music Library, press and hold on a thumbnail until a cross appears and tap once on the cross. However, the item will still be available in iTunes if you want to download it again at a later date.

...cont'd

Full cover view

Cover artwork for songs and albums can be viewed at full-screen size while the songs are being played. You can also view a track list in this view. To do this:

Beware

When your child is listening to any music on the iPad, particularly with headphones, make sure that the sound level is not too high, so as not to damage hearing.

1 While a song is being played, tap once on this icon

2 Tap once on the album cover to show or hide the toolbars

3 For albums, or playlists, swipe left or right to play the next song and display its artwork

Don't forget

Playlists of specific songs can also be created within the Music app. To do this, tap once on the **Playlist** button on the bottom toolbar. Then tap once on the **New** button, give it a name and add songs from the Music Library. Once a playlist has been created it can be accessed from the **Playlist** button.

4 Double-tap to display the track list. Tap once on a track to play it

5 Tap once on this button to return to the main Music app window

Creating Music

For any children who are musically inclined there are several apps for creating music on the iPad. One of the most popular is Apple's GarageBand, which is an iPad app (from the App Store) of the full desktop/laptop version which is contained in the Mac iLife suite. GarageBand enables you to create music with a variety of digital instruments and also include pre-recorded loops.
To create music with GarageBand:

Don't forget

There are other music-making apps in the App Store and also apps to enhance GarageBand.

1 Tap once on this icon

2 Tap once here to create a new music project

No songs exist in the My Songs browser
Tap here to start a new song.

3 Tap once on an instrument to select it as an input device

Don't forget

Swipe left and right to access the different instruments that are available in GarageBand.

4 Tap once on the instrument button to access additional options

Don't forget

Tap once on this button to stop recording a track.

5 Tap once on the red **Record** button and play the instrument to create music with it

...cont'd

6 The track is placed in the main window

7 Tap once on the **Instruments** button or tap once on this button in the bottom left-hand corner to access the instruments again and record another track

8 Individual tracks are placed underneath each other

9 Tap once on the track icon to access the **Delete** or **Duplicate** buttons

10 Swipe this button to show or hide the track controls

11 Use these buttons to, from left to right, go to the start of a project, play a project, record a track and adjust the volume

GarageBand settings

There are options at the right-hand side of the main toolbar for adding pre-recorded loops of music and general settings:

1   Tap once on this button to access the pre-recorded loops of music

2   Tap once on the **Instrument** link above to access options for loops created with different instruments

Don't forget

When a suitable loop has been identified it can be added to a song by dragging it onto the main track window.

3   Tap once on this button to select settings for a selected track

Don't forget

If the Metronome is turned **On** it will play a rhythm when an instrument is being recorded for a track.

4   Tap once on this button to select general settings for GarageBand

...cont'd

Editing tracks

Once tracks have been created they can then be edited in a number of ways. To do this:

 Tap once on a track so that a thick border, with buttons at either end, appears

 Drag on the button to trim the length of the track

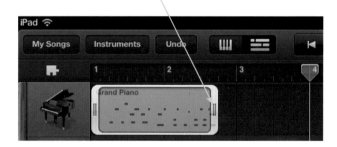

Double-tap on a track to access its menu bar. Use this to **Cut**, **Copy**, **Delete**, **Loop** or **Split** the track

Managing projects

Once projects have been created they can then be managed in the My Songs area. To do this:

1 When you have finished creating or editing a song, tap once on this button

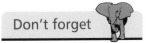

2 Completed projects appear here. Tap once on the name to overwrite it with a new one. Swipe left or right to move between projects

3 Tap once on this button and tap once on the **New Song** button to create a new one

4 Tap once on this button to select and edit completed songs. Tap once on a song to select it

Edit

5 Tap once on this button to share the selected song via sites including Facebook and YouTube

6 Tap once on this button to duplicate the selected song

7 Tap once on this button to delete the selected song. Tap once on the **Done** button once you have finished editing songs in the My Songs section

Playing Games

Computer games are definitely an area where children can be considered experts and they will generally be able to guide adults in terms of obtaining the best games and how to use them. On the iPad there are two main avenues for playing games:

- Through the in-built Game Center app

- With games directly from the App Store

However, parents and teachers should still take a keen interest in games on the iPad and their main areas of concern are:

- Ensuring that children do not spend too long playing games on the iPad at the expense of other activities. This comes down to parental control and the best way is to agree an amount of time that can be spent playing games. There has to be a certain amount of trust involved with this and open discussion is the best way to deal with it rather than turning it into an area of conflict. However, it should also be remembered that there are benefits in playing games, such as hand-eye coordination, concentration, problem solving and social interaction (with multiplayer games)

- Ensuring that children do not access inappropriate content by obtaining games that are not suitable for their age group. Restrictions for this can be put in place within the General section of the Settings app, where age levels can be set for downloading apps (see Chapter Three for details about this)

Within both the Game Center and the App Store there are games for all ages, covering a variety of areas:

- Action

- Adventure

- Arcade

- Puzzles

- Racing

- Role Playing

- Sports

Hot tip

For a lot of games, there are 'cheats' that can be found on the Web. These are tips and shortcuts about achieving higher scores and overcoming particularly difficult obstacles. Children are usually well versed in finding these, frequently through word of mouth from their peers.

Game Center

The Game Center is a built-in iPad app for obtaining and playing games. It can also be used to play games with other people and rate your scores against other Game Center users.
To use the Game Center:

1 Tap once on this icon

2 On the Game Center home screen, enter your Apple ID details and tap once on the **Sign In** button or tap once on the **Create New Account** button to create an account with a new Apple ID

Beware

A lot of standard nicknames are already taken within the Game Center, so you may have to use your name with a selection of numbers and/or symbols.

179

3 Enter a nickname which will appear on scoreboards. If the nickname has already been taken you will be prompted to add another version

4 Drag this button **On** or **Off** to use your contacts for games

5 Tap once on the **Change Photo** button to add a photo for your player profile

...cont'd

Accessing games

Game Center games can be found from the main home screen and also from the Games button. To do this:

 Tap once on one of the game icons on the home screen

 Details of the game are displayed. Tap once on this button to download the game in the same way as for other apps

 **Don't forget**

The Game Center games are part of the main App Store and can be downloaded directly from there too.

Tap once on the **Games** button on the Game Center toolbar

Tap once on this button

Find Game Center Games

Navigate through the Game Center games in the same way as finding any other types of apps

Playing games

When you play games within the Game Center environment you can also compare your scores against other players:

1 Tap once on the **Games** button at the bottom of the Game Center window

2 Tap once on one of your Game Center games

3 Tap once on the **Leaderboard** button to view the high scores for other people playing the same game

Don't forget

To return to the Games section from within the leaderboard, tap once on this button:

181

4 Tap once on the **Play Game** button to access the game

5 Within a Game Center game, tap once on this icon to access the current leaderboard

6 The leaderboard displays the top players, by day, week or all time

...cont'd

Friends and multiplayer games

When you play games within the Game Center environment you can invite friends to compare scores against them and also play multiplayer games. To do this:

1 Tap once on the **Friends** button on the bottom toolbar and tap once on the **Add Friends** button

2 Enter the email address or the nickname of the friend who you want to invite. Tap once on the **Send** button

3 Once a friend has accepted a request, their details will be displayed on the Friends page. This includes the games you have in common and their ranking for these

4 If a game has a multiplayer option, tap once on the Multiplayer button

5 Game Center will find players of an equivalent level so that you can play against them. Tap once on the **Play Now** button to play a multiplayer game

App Store Games

A wide range of games is available in the App Store. These cover a variety of types and also different age groups. To access games:

1   Access the App Store and tap once on the **Games** button

2   The latest featured games are shown in the top panel and others are shown below. Swipe left and right to view more games

Beware

A lot of games that are free to purchase then have offers of items within the game that need to be purchased. These are known as In-App purchases. If you do not want this to be possible, it can be turned off within the **Restrictions** area of the **General** section of the **Settings** app. See Chapter Three for more details about restrictions.

3   Swipe up and down to view currently-popular games and recommendations

4   Tap once on a game to preview it. Download it in the same way as for any other app

Some to try

Choosing games can be very subjective but children are well equipped to find the ones that they like best, partly through word of mouth from their peers. However, here are a few games that provide opportunities for a range of age groups:

- **Ace Rider.** A motorbike racing game with a daring stuntman

- **Angry Birds.** One of the top iPad games, involving the angry birds trying to destroy greedy pigs

- **DragonVale.** For younger children, a role playing game where you have to raise and breed your own dragons

- **Grand Theft Auto.** One of the most popular games in computing history, featuring the activities in Liberty City

- **Jump Birdy Jump.** Another game for younger children, featuring a bird who has to collect stars to join his partner

- **Kingdom Rush.** A fantasy defence game where you have to protect your kingdom against orcs, trolls, wizards and more

- **NFL Flick Quarterback.** For any fans of American football

- **Peppa Pig's Party Time.** Play party games with this game featuring the popular cartoon character

- **Quell.** A puzzle game suitable for most ages where you move around various screens, collecting pearls

- **Scrabble for iPad.** An iPad version of the popular word game

- **Sliding Tiles.** An educational game consisting of puzzles where you move pieces to complete various tasks

- **Tap Pet Shop.** Create your own pet shop and look after animals so that customers can adopt them

- **Temple Run.** A simple but addictive game where you have to run as far as you can through a temple of obstacles

- **Tiny Zoo Friends.** A simulation game for younger children to collect, and care for, zoo animals

- **Where's My Water.** A series of puzzles that stress the environmental importance of preserving water

Drawing and Painting Apps

When famous artists start using painting and drawing apps on the iPad you know that this is a serious option for creating pictures. The artist David Hockney is a well known exponent of the iPad and has produced some stunning artwork with it. Even if you are not an internationally renowned artist, there are some great options for drawing and painting on the iPad. This can be done just for pleasure, or they can be used to produce diagrams for school work. To use drawing and painting apps (these examples are for the Drawing Pad app, but the functionality is similar for most drawing and painting apps):

1 Tap on one of the options on the main menu. Tap once on **New** to create a new painting

185

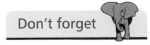

Don't forget

David Hockney uses the Brushes app for creating his artwork.

2 Tap once on one of the drawing or painting tools

3 The full range for a tool is displayed. Tap once to select a tool

4 Swipe left and right to move between the available tools

...cont'd

5 Drag on the screen to create a picture

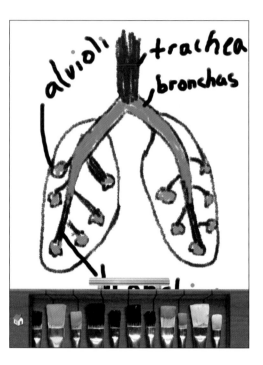

Hot tip

If you want to hide the main toolbar in drawing and painting apps, to give you more space for your picture, this can usually be done by swiping on the button at the top of the toolbar.

6 Tap once on the **Save** option to access options for saving, printing and sharing the picture

7 Tap once on the **Menu** button to return to the home screen at any time

8 Tap once on the **Album** button to view the pictures that have been created

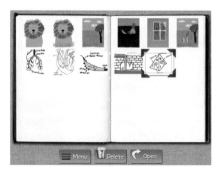

9 Communicating

The iPad has numerous options for communicating and this chapter shows how to do this, via the Web, email, messaging and video.

Getting Connected

Accessing the Internet is a key part of communication on the iPad. Not only does it provide access to the Web and email, it also ensures connection to the App Store and apps including iTunes, Videos and Maps. iPads connect to the Internet via Wi-Fi: if it is in the home it will connect to this automaticallly once it has been set up; if it is in a public Wi-Fi area it will ask which network you would like to join. To connect to a Wi-Fi network:

1 Tap once on this icon

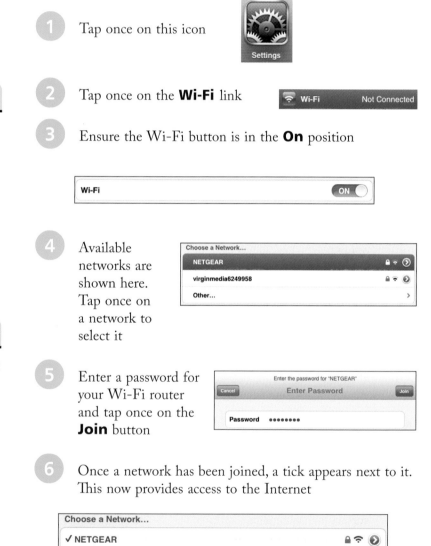

Don't forget

When you enter a password for a Wi-Fi router, you can also use the **Join** button on the iPad keyboard.

188

2 Tap once on the **Wi-Fi** link

3 Ensure the Wi-Fi button is in the **On** position

4 Available networks are shown here. Tap once on a network to select it

Beware

If a padlock appears next to a network it indicates it is a secure network, i.e. one that requires a password before you can join it. If there is no padlock it is unsecured which means that it could be easier for other people to hack into your iPad, if they are that way inclined. However, it is still unlikely to happen.

5 Enter a password for your Wi-Fi router and tap once on the **Join** button

6 Once a network has been joined, a tick appears next to it. This now provides access to the Internet

Using Safari

The Safari app is the default web browser on the iPad. This can be used to view web pages, save favorites and read pages with the Reader function. To use Safari:

1 Tap once on this icon

2 Tap once on the Address Bar and type a web page address. Suggested options appear as you type

3 Tap once on the **Go** button on the keyboard to open the web page

4 The selected web page opens in Safari. Swipe up and down and left and right to navigate around the page

5 Tap once here on the **Share** button to access options for bookmarking a page, adding it to the reading list to view at a later time, adding an icon to the home screen for quick access to the page, emailing or tweeting the link for the page and printing it

Don't forget

There are other browser apps for the iPad, including Chrome, Atomic, Opera, Mercury Skyfire and Dolphin. There is also Mobicip Safe Browser which can restrict certain types of content (see page 59).

Don't forget

Double-tap with one finger on a web page to zoom in on it. Double-tap again to return to normal view.

Hot tip

Press and hold on an image on a web page to access options to **Save** or **Copy**.

...cont'd

6 Tap once here to view the history of visited web pages

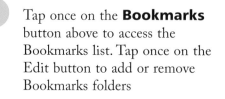

7 Tap once on the **Bookmarks** button above to access the Bookmarks list. Tap once on the Edit button to add or remove Bookmarks folders

Don't forget

If you have iCloud set up on another Mac computer, or mobile device, you will be able to synchronize your bookmarks in Safari on your iPad. To do this you must have iCloud set up for this on the iPad, which can be done within **Settings > iCloud**.

8 Tap once here to open a new tab for another web page

9 The page is opened in the new tab. Tap once on the tab headings to move between pages

Hot tip

To open a web link in a new tab, press and hold on it and tap once on **Open in New Tab**, rather than just tapping on it.

10 In the Address Bar, if the Reader button appears it means the page can be read without the distraction of other content

11 Tap once on the **Reader** button to view the page in this format. Tap once on the button again to return to the standard page format

Safari settings

Settings for Safari can be specified in the Settings app. To do this:

1 Tap once on this icon

2 Tap once on the **Safari** link

3 General options are shown here for selecting a search engine, filling in forms, tabs and bookmarks

General	
Search Engine	Google >
AutoFill	Names and Passwords >
Open New Tabs in Background	ON
Always Show Bookmarks Bar	ON

4 Drag the **Private Browsing** button **Off** to disable this

Privacy	
Private Browsing	OFF
Accept Cookies	From visited >

5 Tap once on the **Accept Cookies** link to specify how Safari deals with cookies from websites

6 Tap once on **Clear History** and **Clear Cookies and Data** to remove these items

Clear History
Clear Cookies and Data

7 Drag this button to **On** to enable alerts for when you have visited a fraudulent website

Security	
Fraud Warning	ON

8 Drag these buttons **On** to enable Javascript files on websites and also block pop-up messages

JavaScript	ON
Block Pop-ups	ON

Email on the iPad

Email on the iPad is sent and received using the Mail app. This provides a range of functionality for managing email. To use this:

1 Tap once on this icon (the red icon in the corner displays the number of unread emails)

2 Tap once on a message to display it in the main panel

3 Use these buttons to, from left to right, move a message, delete a message, respond to a message and create a new message

4 Tap once on this button and then Reply to a message, Forward it to a new recipient, Save an Image in a message or Print it

5 Tap once on this button to create a new message

6 Enter a recipient, subject and body text. Tap once on the **Send** button

Mailboxes

Different categories of email messages can be managed via mailboxes. For instance, your child may want to keep their social emails separately from ones that apply to school activities. To use different mailboxes:

1 Tap once on the **Mailboxes** button

2 The current mailboxes are displayed. Tap once on the **Edit** button

3 Tap once on the **New Mailbox** button at the bottom of the Mailboxes panel

4 Enter a name for the new mailbox and tap once on the **Save** button

5 Tap once on the **Done** button

6 To delete a mailbox, tap on it once at Step 3, instead of the New Mailbox button, and tap on the **Delete Mailbox** button

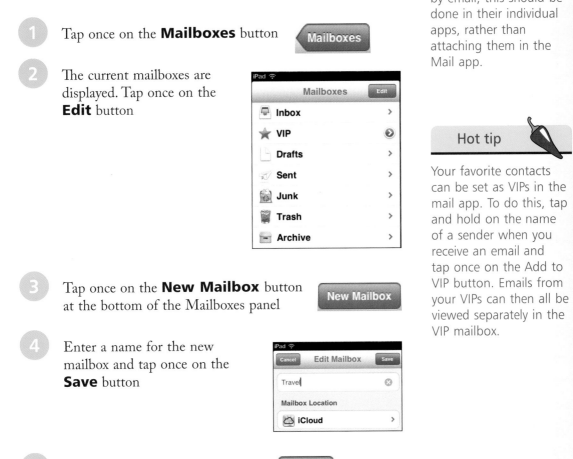

Hot tip

If you want to share files by email, this should be done in their individual apps, rather than attaching them in the Mail app.

Hot tip

Your favorite contacts can be set as VIPs in the mail app. To do this, tap and hold on the name of a sender when you receive an email and tap once on the Add to VIP button. Emails from your VIPs can then all be viewed separately in the VIP mailbox.

Don't forget

To go back to your Inbox from the mailboxes, tap once on the **Inbox** link after Step 5.

193

Email threads

When you receive a number of emails on the same subject, they can be sorted into threads, for easier viewing. To do this:

 If there is an email thread, there is a number next to each email

 Tap once on the email to view the items in the full thread

The Threads function can be turned On and Off in the Settings app under the Mail, Contacts, Calendars link. In the Mail section, drag the Organize by Thread button On or Off.

Tap once on an individual email in the thread to view its contents

Editing Mailboxes

Messages can be edited within individual mailboxes. To do this:

Tap once on a mailbox

Hot tip

Individual emails can also be deleted from mailboxes by swiping on them from right to left and tapping once on the Delete button.

Tap once on the **Edit** button

Tap once next to a message to select it and tap once on one of the Delete, Move or Mark options at the bottom of the panel

Email settings and accounts

Email settings can be specified within the Settings app.
Different email accounts can also be added here.

1 Tap once on this icon

2 Tap once on the **Mail, Contacts, Calendars** link

📧	Mail, Contacts, Calendars

3 Under the Mail section there are several options for how Mail operates and looks. These include the number of messages being displayed, previewing emails and font size

Mail	
Show	50 Recent Messages >
Preview	2 Lines >
Show To/Cc Label	OFF
Ask Before Deleting	OFF
Load Remote Images	ON
Organize By Thread	ON
Always Bcc Myself	OFF
Increase Quote Level	On >
Signature	Sent from my iPad >
Default Account	iCloud >

4 Tap once on the **Add Account** link to add a new account

Accounts	
iCloud Mail, Contacts, Calendars, Bookmarks, Reminders, Notes, Photo Stream, Documents & Data, Backup	>
Add Account...	>

5 Tap once on the type of email account you want to add

10:40   Add Account...

- ☁ iCloud
- 🪟 Microsoft Exchange
- Gmail
- YAHOO!

6 Enter the details for the account. Tap once on the **Next** button to complete the account setup process

Cancel	Gmail	Next
Name	John Appleseed	
Address	example@gmail.com	
Password	Required	
Description	My Gmail Account	

Hot tip

One of the Mail settings is for changing the email signature, i.e. the message that appears automatically at the bottom of each email. By default it says **Sent from my iPad**. To change this, tap once on the **Signature** link and type a new signature message.

195

iMessage

In addition to email, another option for communication is the Apple iMessage service that is accessed via the Messages app. This enables text and photo messages to be sent, free of charge, between users of the iOS 6 operating system, on the iPad, iPhone and iPod Touch, and the OS X operating system (from Lion onwards). iMessages can be sent to cell/mobile phone numbers and email addresses. To use iMessages:

1 Tap once on this icon

2 Enter details for your location and your email address. Tap once on the **Next** button

Beware

If a number, or email address, is not recognized it shows up in red in the To: box.

3 Tap once on this button to create a new message and start a new conversation

4 Enter a phone number, or email address, here (this has to belong to an iOS 6 or Mac user)

5 Tap once on this button to select someone from your contacts

6 Tap once on a contact to select them as the recipient of the new message

Creating iMessages

To create and edit messages and conversations:

1 Tap once here and type with the keyboard to create a message. Tap once on the **Send** button

Hot tip

To include a photo or a video, tap once on the camera icon in Step 1 and select the required item from within the Photos app, or capture a new photo or video.

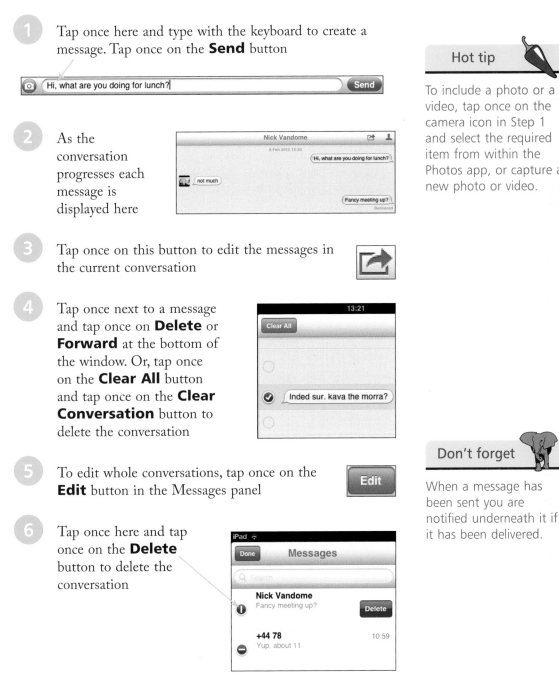

2 As the conversation progresses each message is displayed here

3 Tap once on this button to edit the messages in the current conversation

4 Tap once next to a message and tap once on **Delete** or **Forward** at the bottom of the window. Or, tap once on the **Clear All** button and tap once on the **Clear Conversation** button to delete the conversation

5 To edit whole conversations, tap once on the **Edit** button in the Messages panel

Don't forget

When a message has been sent you are notified underneath it if it has been delivered.

6 Tap once here and tap once on the **Delete** button to delete the conversation

Social Networking

Young people have always found ways to interact with their peers and the Internet has now provided a virtual means to do this through social networking sites. These are websites and text messaging services that link people so that they can share information, photos, thoughts, opinions, jokes and almost anything else that they want to. As with any new technology, there were originally a number of players in the social networking market. But this has now been consolidated to two main players: Facebook and Twitter.

Facebook

This is now the most widely-used social networking tool and it offers a range of functionality: To use Facebook you have to first register, which is free. You can then link up with your friends by searching for them and inviting them with a Friend Request. You can also be invited by other people and you have to accept their request before you can be friends. The types of things you can do on Facebook are:

- Posting of status messages – telling the world what you have been doing or your opinions about things

- Adding photos

- Commenting on your friends' posts and photos

- Private messaging. Sending private messages to your friends

- Creating and joining groups of people with similar interests and hobbies

Facebook can be accessed on your iPad through the website on Safari. However, there is also a Facebook app that can be downloaded from the App Store which is designed for mobile access to Facebook.

Don't forget

See Chapter Three for details about security issues on Facebook.

Facebook
Facebook, Inc.

Social Networ...
★★☆☆☆ (1.012)

Twitter

Twitter is a relatively new social networking tool, launched in 2006, but it has grown at a remarkable rate and is now one of the most visited websites in the world. It is a microblogging site where users post short messages, of up to 140 characters.
Once you have joined Twitter you can follow other users to see what they are saying and have people follow you too. To use Twitter on your iPad

1 Tap once on this icon

2 Tap once on the **Twitter** link

3 Tap once on the **Install** button to install the Twitter app

4 In the Twitter Settings, tap once on the **Create New Account** button

Don't forget

A message on Twitter is known as a tweet.

5 Enter the required account details and tap once on the **Sign Up** button

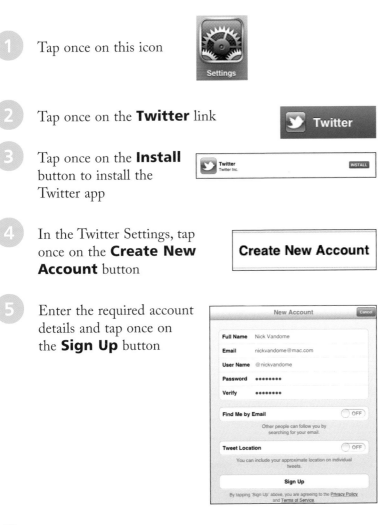

6 Tap once on this icon to access Twitter through the iPad Twitter app

...cont'd

Using Twitter

Once you have registered for Twitter you can start using it:

1 Tap once on the **Search** button to find other users to follow

2 Type a name in the Search box to find a user

3 Select a Twitter user and tap once here to **Follow** them

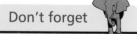
4 When you follow someone, their tweets will show up on your homepage and your Timeline

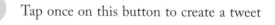

5 Tap once on this button to create a tweet

6 Type your tweet and tap once on the **Send** button

7 Your tweet appears on your homepage and timeline.

Anyone who is following you will be able to see it too

Using FaceTime

Communicating with text is a fast and efficient way of keeping in touch, but there are times when you can't beat seeing each other. The FaceTime app provides this facility with video chatting with other iOS 6 users on the iPad, iPhone and iPod Touch, or a Mac computer with FaceTime. To use FaceTime for video chatting:

1 Tap once on this icon

Don't forget

FaceTime has to be turned on in the **FaceTime** section of the **Settings** app.

2 Sign in using your Apple ID to create your FaceTime account

3 Tap once on the **Contacts** button

4 Tap once on a contact to access their details for making a FaceTime call

5 Tap once on their phone number or email address to make a FaceTime call. The recipient must have FaceTime on their iPad, iPhone, iPod Touch or Mac computer

6 Tap once on the **Add to Favorites** button to add the contact to your favorites list so that it can be accessed quickly

...cont'd

7 Once you have selected a contact, FaceTime starts connecting to them and displays this button

Hot tip

The contacts for FaceTime calls are taken from the iPad Contacts app. You can also add new contacts directly to the contacts list by tapping once on the + sign and adding the relevant details for the new contact.

8 When you have connected, your contact appears in the main window and you appear in a picture-in-picture thumbnail in the corner

Don't forget

You can move your own picture-in-picture thumbnail to different corners of the screen.

9 Tap once on this button to swap between cameras on your iPad

10 Tap once on this button to end the FaceTime call

11 If someone else makes a call to you, tap once on the **Decline** or **Accept** buttons

10 Sharing with the iPad

This chapter shows how to back up, transfer and share files on your iPad.

Using iCloud

iCloud is the Apple service for storing and backing up items on your iPad. It can also be used to make photos, videos, music, settings and data available across other Apple devices, including other iPads, iPhones, iPod Touches (with iOS 5 or later) and iMacs and MacBooks with OS X Lion (10.7.2 or later) installed.

When your iPad is connected to the Internet over Wi-Fi, iCloud will back up the following items automatically if the iPad is connected to a power source and is locked:

- Purchased music, TV shows, apps and books
- Photos
- Settings and app data
- Messages

With an iCloud account you get a free email account and 5 GB of storage for documents and backup. You can also purchase extra storage if required.

Once iCloud has been set up it takes care of all of the saving, backing up and synchronizing issues so you don't have to worry about it.

iCloud Settings
To set up iCloud:

Beware

iCloud only backs up music purchased from iTunes. If you have imported any of your own music via iTunes this will not be backed up.

Hot tip

Your iCloud account can be accessed online from any Internet-enabled computer at www.icloud.com

1 Tap once on this icon

2 Tap once on the **iCloud** link

3 Tap once here to create a new iCloud account or view the details of an existing one

iCloud	
Account	nickvandome@mac.com >

4 Drag these buttons to the **On** position for all of the items you would like to include in iCloud. These items will be backed up automatically by iCloud

✉ Mail	ON ⬤
👤 Contacts	ON ⬤
📅 Calendars	ON ⬤
📝 Reminders	ON ⬤
🧭 Safari	ON ⬤
📄 Notes	ON ⬤
🌸 Photo Stream	On >
📁 Documents & Data	On >
🧭 Find My iPad	ON ⬤

5 Tap once on the **My Photo Stream** link and drag the button

Photo Stream

My Photo Stream   ON ⬤

Automatically upload new photos and send them to all of your iCloud devices when connected to Wi-Fi.

to **On** to enable iCloud to copy your photos and make them available to other compatible devices

6 Tap once on **Documents & Data** link and drag

Documents & Data   ON ⬤

Allow apps to store documents and data in iCloud.

the button to **On** to copy your documents to iCloud

7 Tap once on the **Storage & Backup** link

📦 Storage & Backup   >

8 Tap once on the **Change Storage Plan** link to view how your storage

Storage	
Total Storage	25.0 GB
Available	23.3 GB
Manage Storage	>
Change Storage Plan	

is being used and add more if required

Don't forget

Tap once on the **Change Storage Plan** link to upgrade your iCloud storage. Above 5GB there is a charge, depending on how much storage you require.

Backing up with iCloud

Not only can iCloud store the content from your iPad and make it available to other devices, it can also back it up in case it is deleted or your iPad is lost or destroyed. Data stored on iCloud can then be restored, either to your original iPad, or even a new device. To back up with iCloud:

1 Access the iCloud section of the Settings app and tap once on the **Storage & Backup** link

Storage & Backup	>

2 Drag the **iCloud Backup** button to **On**

Backup

iCloud Backup   ON

Automatically back up your camera roll, accounts, documents, and settings when this iPad is plugged in, locked, and connected to Wi-Fi.

Back Up Now

Last Backup: 11:22

3 Tap once on the **Back Up Now** link. iCloud will then back up your data automatically when it is connected to a power source and locked

4 If you ever need to restore the data to your iPad, or to another device, restart the device and tap once on the **Restore from iCloud Backup** link, rather than the Set Up as New iPad link. This will then restore all of the data from the iCloud backup

Set Up as New iPad	✓
Restore from iCloud Backup	
Restore from iTunes Backup	

Beware

If you want to test the restore process you can do so by resetting your iPad under the **General** section of the **Settings** app, by tapping once on the **Reset** link and then **Erase All Content and Settings**. However, if there is no need to do it then it is best not to.

Managing Storage

When you are backing up the content on your iPad to iCloud you can specify manually which items are included in the backup. This is done in the Storage & Backup section as shown on the previous page. To manage your iCloud storage:

1 In **Storage & Backup** section, tap once on the **Manage Storage** link

Storage	
Total Storage	25.0 GB
Available	23.3 GB
Manage Storage	›

2 Tap once on your iPad's name in the **Backups** section. (Underneath this there are details of iWork apps that store documents and data in iCloud. Tap once on each to see what specific files are being stored)

Backups	1.3 GB
My iPad black	710.7 MB ›
iPad _This iPad_	631.6 MB ›
Documents & Data	25.6 MB
Pages	23 MB ›
Numbers	1.4 MB ›
Keynote	1.3 MB ›
Mail	
Mail	345.6 MB

3 Backup details are displayed at the top of the window, underneath the iPad's name. Drag these buttons **On** or **Off** to include, or exclude, apps in the iCloud backup. If they are dragged **Off**, any previously-backed up data will be deleted

iPad _This iPad_	
Latest Backup	Yesterday
Backup Size	611 MB
Backup Options Choose the data you want to back up.	
Next Backup Size	635 MB
Camera Roll _494 MB_	ON
Drawing Pad _19.8 MB_	OFF
Evernote _16.1 MB_	ON
Keynote _12.4 MB_	ON
GarageBand _12.3 MB_	ON
Show All Apps	
Delete Backup	

Beware

If you select the **Delete Backup** button in Step 3 this will delete all of the information that has been previously backed up to iCloud. It is not recommended that this is done, unless you have a good reason to do so.

Sharing with iTunes

Items on your iPad can be shared via other computers using iTunes. This can include synchronizing music, movies, books, photos and apps. You can also share documents that you have created on your iPad, if the other computer has compatible apps for viewing and editing them.

Syncing with iTunes

Synchronization with your iPad and iTunes can either be done over Wi-Fi or with the USB Lightning Connector cable that comes with the iPad. To do this:

Beware

Music and photos can take up a lot of storage space and could quickly fill up your iPad if you sync them from another computer. For both of these options you can select just to sync selected items, rather than your entire music or photo libraries. This is done in the panels for each item.

Hot tip

To sync over Wi-Fi, scroll down in the **Summary** panel. Under **Options**, check on the **Sync with this iPad over Wi-Fi** box.

1. Connect the iPad to the other computer and open iTunes on that computer

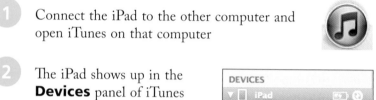

2. The iPad shows up in the **Devices** panel of iTunes

3. Set up the iPad ready for synchronizing. Select any items you want synced automatically

4. The Summary panel displays general information about the iPad

5. Tap once on the main toolbar to select the items that you want to sync

6 Tap once next to the items you want to sync

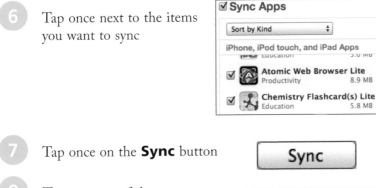

7 Tap once on the **Sync** button

8 The progress of the synchronization is displayed at the top of the iTunes window

An iPad can be synced with iTunes on either a Mac computer or a Windows one.

Transferring files

Files can be transferred from your iPad to another computer, and vice versa, using iTunes. First you have to save the iPad files to iTunes and then you can transfer them to compatible apps on another computer with iTunes. To do this:

1 In an appropriate app, tap once on the tools button and tap once on the **Share and Print** link

2 Tap once on the **Copy to iTunes** link

3 Select a format in which you want to transfer the document

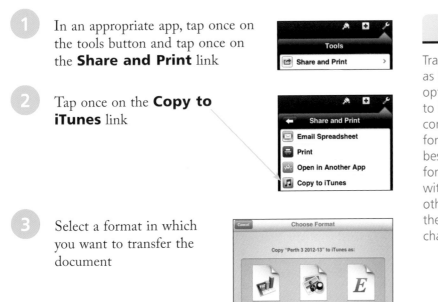

Transferring documents as PDF files is a good option for allowing them to be viewed on other computers. However, for editing purposes it is best to save them in a format that is compatible with an app on the other computer, so that they can be opened and changed.

...cont'd

 Tap once on the **Apps** button on the top toolbar

Scroll down to the File Sharing section and select an app

In order to share documents with iTunes, the app has to support this function. Check an app's Help file (if it has one) to see whether it supports iTunes sharing.

File Sharing
The apps listed below can transfer documents between your iPad and this computer.

Apps	Keynote Documents
IntellectivePhysics	Presentation.key Today 17:53
Keynote	
Kindle	

Tap once on a document

Tap once on **Save to...** button and select a location on your computer where you would like to save the document

Save to...

Tap once on **Add...** button to select a file and add it to the iPad

Add...

In an app on the iPad, tap here and select **Copy from iTunes**, to open a document that has been copied from another computer with iTunes

+

Create Document

Copy from iTunes

Copy from WebDAV

Tap once on the document that you want to copy

Cancel   Copy from iTunes

iPad security
11 Feb 2012 16:43

Facebook
11 Feb 2012 16:42

Hot tip

Photos and videos can be transferred to a Windows PC by connecting with the Lightning cable connector and accessing the iPad through File Explorer and then copying and pasting the required files.

Index

S